Inclusivity and Tru
the Classroom

Drawing from a wealth of specialist and mainstream school experience, this book intelligently synthesises ground-breaking research on teacher–student trust and learning to present innovative approaches to inclusive practice relevant to practitioners at all levels. Relational trust has critical implications for student engagement and learning, and new findings contribute insightfully to teacher approaches which are invaluable for practitioners at any stage of their career. The components of relational trust are clearly explained in this essential resource. Each theme is accompanied by a range of useful strategies which enable practitioners to deploy trust theory to develop a more sustainable education system. This thoughtful approach has the potential to shift educational priorities and advance equitable access to education for all students.

Victoria Byrnell is a teacher with extensive experience in inclusive education.

To Mike,

"the scholarship of love is
to serve in all we do" (p116)

All best wishes

Inclusivity and Trust in the Classroom

Helping the Child in Front of You to Learn and Thrive

Victoria Byrnell

Routledge
Taylor & Francis Group

LONDON AND NEW YORK

Designed cover image: Photograph of Spiral Poppy Long by Adam Krajewski, August 2019, Mixed media

First published 2025
by Routledge
4 Park Square, Milton Park, Abingdon, Oxon OX14 4RN

and by Routledge
605 Third Avenue, New York, NY 10158

Routledge is an imprint of the Taylor & Francis Group, an informa business

British Library Cataloguing-in-Publication Data
A catalogue record for this book is available from the British Library

ISBN: 978-1-032-73961-8 (hbk)
ISBN: 978-1-032-73960-1 (pbk)
ISBN: 978-1-003-46696-3 (ebk)

DOI: 10.4324/9781003466963

Typeset in Sabon
by KnowledgeWorks Global Ltd.

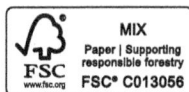

MIX
Paper | Supporting
responsible forestry
FSC
www.fsc.org   FSC® C013056

Printed and bound in Great Britain by
TJ Books, Padstow, Cornwall

To educators and students, this book is written for you.

To Carla

Contents

Preface

This book originated over a decade ago when I was the deputy head-teacher of a secondary special school where the practice I encountered was so shocking I struggled to comprehend it. It transpired there were grounds for whistleblowing, a career-risking process which was set to fail but for a timely visit from the Office for Standards in Education (Ofsted) for whom a red dot next to the school had indicated an internal inspection process, prompting them to dig deeper. The lead inspector shared with me that the process had been like 'peeling the layers of an onion which was rotten to its core' and whilst I am aware of misgivings about Ofsted, in this instance they did their job well.

Towards the end of an extended interregnum working with a series of interim headteachers, I decided to inject some positivity and set up a working party to write a new school mission statement. At that time, one of the categories for students with special educational needs was behaviour, social and emotional difficulties (BESD); invariably many students also had additional learning needs, and I used to refer to them affectionately as 'BLESD'. I suggested themes for the new mission statement using the acronym BLESSINGS, and my colleagues enthusiastically adopted the idea of *blessings for the blesd*. Readers may notice that the acronym BLESSINGS can be found in the chapters of Part I, and the majority of themes remain unchanged from all those years ago, albeit my experience, research and understandings have evolved.

I was fortunate that my time at this school where the seeds of Inclusivity and Trust in the Classroom were sown ended well, eventually working alongside an insightful and experienced headteacher to lift the school out of special measures. Subsequently, I returned to mainstream education where my career-long drive to improve the life-chances of systemically vulnerable students through educational inclusion has been purposeful and rewarding, providing many more fulfilling years in a profession I hold in high esteem.

Ultimately, my research journey to discover more about teacher–student trust was the turning point which compelled me to revisit my book to share my learnings and empower practitioners in their inclusive practice. A colleague once described systemically vulnerable students as being 'hidden under stones'. Similarities can be drawn between unturning the stones at the aforementioned school which enabled it to change and thrive, and uncovering the human stones of distrust, which when combined with trust practice, arguably have the potential to transform education for all.

Acknowledgements

My sincere thanks to all the student research participants, for your commitment to the process and for your authenticity and insight which contribute to the professional understanding of teacher-student trust. To Professor Brené Brown, sincere thanks for your seminal social science research which enabled a deeper understanding of my research findings and their links with key themes in this book. To Dr Mary Milovilovic, thank you for your wisdom, humour and expert tutelage during my time at St Mary's. To my long-time colleagues and friends, Kate Bennett and Chris Willis, thank you for your steadfast support, encouragement and input over the years. Lastly to my partner George, this book would not be written without your unwavering patience, kindness and belief which are etched in my heart.

Acronyms

ADHD	Attention-deficit hyperactivity disorder
CATs	Cognitive Ability Tests
DFE	Department for Education
EHCP	Educational Health and Care Plan
EL	Emotional literacy/intelligence
GCSE	General Certificate of Secondary Education
INSET	In-Service Education and Training
MAT	Multi Academy Trust
OECD	Organisation for Economic Co-operation and Development
OFSTED	Office for Standards in Education
SATs	Standard Assessment Tests
SEAL	Social and Emotional Aspects of Learning
SEMH	Social, Emotional and Mental Health
SEND	Special educational needs and disabilities
SENDCo	Special Educational Needs Co-ordinator
SOLE	Self-orientated learning environments

All names used in this book have been changed to protect anonymity.

Part I

1 Introduction

Evidence points to increasing challenges in delivering inclusive education to diverse student populations. On a daily basis, a classroom of 35 children are told to permanently leave mainstream schools, and although not unprecedented, pre-pandemic exclusion rates rose by 60% over five years.[1] Post-pandemic, data suggests both permanent and fixed term exclusions continue to rise and that school absence is significantly higher among systemically vulnerable groups.[2] *Special Educational Needs and Disabilities (SEND), poverty, ethnicity, being bullied, poor teacher relationships, trauma, challenges in home life* and *low attainment* are all factors which impact student inclusion.[3]

The legacy of UK educational reform in the 1990s is a system driven by standardisation, accountability, competition and equality which has arguably frustrated *equitable* educational provision. Government publications acknowledge a prevailing climate of inequality across disadvantaged student populations,[4] and the relationship between socioeconomic status and reading remains lower than the Organisation for Economic Co-operation and Development (OECD) average.[5] Across the country, student disadvantage gaps are wide-ranging, from 0.5 to 26.3 months, with recent data modelling suggesting the gap at General Certificate of Secondary Education (GCSE) is no longer closing at all.[6] In the existing climate of resource scarcity and fragmentation, the term *inclusion* is at risk of contamination, increasingly associated with 'lack of funding, time, and supports'.[7] Across three decades as a dedicated inclusion specialist in state-maintained schools, I am keenly aware that inclusion can be a contentious issue as practitioners seek to meet the educational needs of all students in an increasingly pressurised system.

Alongside the macro educational context, experience points to the issue of *relationship breakdown* as an occupational challenge which has a critical effect on inclusion, often impacting disproportionately on systemically vulnerable students. It is suggested that 90% of internal difficulties faced by organisations are attributable to dysfunctional relationships among people[8] with the detrimental effect of relationship

DOI: 10.4324/9781003466963-2

breakdown on teacher morale and retention also acknowledged by the Office for Standards in Education (OFSTED).[9] As a senior leader in a school where long-term relational dysfunction had resulted in cover-ups, collusion and malpractice I have seen firsthand how damaging the impacts can be across multiple stakeholder groups. Although cases of relational dysfunction are seldom so entrenched, experience suggests that pockets exist in many schools which remain difficult to diagnose or address. Whilst there may be a tendency to attribute individual accountability, arguably we all share responsibility for problems generated within a system.[10]

In 2019, I completed a master's degree in Education with a research focus on teacher-student trust development. Ultimately, my findings were like completing a jigsaw puzzle where I had been staring at the missing pieces for years but never quite worked out how they slotted together. Whilst there are always new puzzles to be solved, the question this book seeks to address is *how best to equip practitioners* to promote *inclusive, trusting classrooms and schools which maximise educationally desirable outcomes for every student?* If there is genuine commitment to inclusion for all students, then educationally desirable outcomes arguably need to be broader than those generated by 'a narrow test-focused system' which 'confuses test scores with quality of education'.[11] I hope that the learnings and strategies provided in this book facilitate changes in thinking and practice to realise broader educational aims encompassing the values, approaches and skills that enable young people to learn and thrive across all educational settings. Serving the best interests of children is to serve the best interests of humanity[12] which is feasibly a calling all educational practitioners can aspire to.

Notes

1 Boddington L (2020). 'Invisible Girls: Why School Exclusions Are Not Gender Neutral', Social Finance UK, https://medium.com/social-finance-uk/invisible-girls-why-school-exclusions-are-not-gender-neutral-fa732d64c1a9. Accessed 17.11.21.
2 DFE (2023). 'Suspension and Permanent Exclusion from Maintained Schools, Academies and Pupil Referral Units in England, Including Pupil Movement', https://assets.publishing.service.gov.uk/government/uploads/system/uploads/attachment_data/file/1181584/Suspension_and_permanent_exclusion_guidance_september_23.pdf. Accessed 10.09.23.
3 The Secretary of State for Education (2019). 'The Timpson Review of School Exclusion', https://assets.publishing.service.gov.uk/government/uploads/system/uploads/attachment_data/file/807862/Timpson_review.pdf. Accessed 11.06.21.
4 HM Government (2022). 'SEND Review: Right Support, Right Place, Right Time', Department for Education; Department of Health and Social Care.

5 Organisation for Economic Co-operation and Development (2018). 'Programme for International Student Assessment (PIZA) 2018 Results', https://www.oecd.org/pisa/publications/pisa-2018-results.htm. Accessed 05.11.21.

6 Education Policy Institute, in partnership with the Fair Education Alliance (2020). 'Education in England: Annual Report 2020', https://epi.org.uk/publications-and-research/education-in-england-annual-report-2020/. Accessed 09.02.2022.

7 Moore S (2016, p. 4). 'One without the Other: Stories of Unity through Diversity and Inclusion', Porter & Main Press.

8 Seagal S & Horne D (2018). 'Human Dynamics for the 21st Century', Human Dynamics Institute, https://thesystemsthinker.com/human-dynamics-for-the-21st-century/. Accessed 15.12.21.

9 OFSTED (2019). 'Education Inspection Framework: Overview of Research', No. 180045. https://www.gov.uk/government/publications/education-inspection-framework-overview-of-research. Accessed 24.02.25.

10 Senge PM (2006). 'The Fifth Discipline: The Art and Practice of the Learning Organisation', Random House Business Books.

11 Aynsley-Green A (2019, p. 148). 'The British Betrayal of Childhood: Challenging Uncomfortable Truths and Bringing About Change', Routledge.

12 Carol Bellamy (undated). 'Executive Director of the United Nations Children's Fund (UNICEF) from 1995'.

2   Belonging to Yourself

Research evidence suggests that *connection* and *belonging* are embedded in the human genetic code observed at both neural and peripheral biological levels.[1] Connection and belonging are fundamental human needs closely linked with a range of positive outcomes relating to higher academic performance, resilience and health.[2] Ensuring students learn to build the skills required to connect with others in schools is vital, not only because social disconnection is becoming more prevalent across developed cultures but also because the struggle to belong is greater for marginalised groups.[3] Connection and belonging are essential features of relational trust and inclusion and it is important to pay attention to a paradox inherent in the concept of belonging which is often overlooked. The paradox of belonging is that it involves both the desire to connect and belong to something greater than ourselves, but also *the confidence to stand alone and be true to who we are.*[4] Thus, students need to develop a healthy sense of belonging to both the school community and *themselves*, regardless of their imperfections, histories, and unfinished potential. Developing the confidence to be authentic to oneself is the truest sense of belonging which enables meaningful connection with others.[5]

True belonging requires people to believe unquestionably that although flawed and imperfect, they are nevertheless *valued*, *loved* and *good enough* regardless of their critics, situations or shortcomings. To a greater or lesser extent, most people struggle with authentic belonging and naturally gravitate towards the comfort of familiar environments and people where they can be themselves, connect and feel accepted. For young people, the struggle for belonging is often greatest and rooted in both home and school environments. It is salient that teachers are second only to parents in the level of influence they exert over young people whose sense of belonging can be dented when they[6]:

- fail to meet teacher expectations,
- are not able to master the skills teachers want them to master,
- are disliked, unpopular or sidelined.

DOI: 10.4324/9781003466963-3

High expectations, achievement and popularity are common aspirations of both parents and teachers, but it can be easy to miss the fact that for many students, falling short of these aspirations dents their perceptions of value and lovability. Lack of achievement or disappointing others commonly triggers feelings of human inadequacy, but arguably goals and expectations can only be met if students are provided with the stepping stones they need along the way. Developing a sense of authentic belonging is an important stepping stone to overcome the challenges students will invariably encounter in their school and life experiences.

There is a need to distinguish between *belonging* and *fitting in* because the thirst for belonging is so fundamental it can inadvertently drive people to try and fit in and seek approval[7]; students, for example, often seek to please and fit in. However, fitting in and seeking approval are deceptive substitutes for belonging which is only possible when people feel safe to be themselves without fear of judgement. Reciprocal connection and true belonging are compromised in the face of anxiety about how others may think or respond, and this is particularly the case for young people who are still in the process of *becoming*. School systems inherently promote fitting in cultures which are hard to combat unless there is recognition that flexibility, difference and inclusivity are essential for imperfect, diverse communities of people to thrive. Routines, rules and expectations build self-discipline and sustain order which are important but living organisations like trees need to bend in the wind to survive which may require expedient adaptations to be considered. The problem is that in some schools *conformity* is a *prerequisite* for acceptance and belonging and responses to nonconformance can create alienation rather than enabling students to develop self-acceptance and self-discipline as a result of genuine, authentic human connection with trusted adults.[8]

Students who lack a healthy sense of belonging are often hungry for *attention, approval* and *affection* (in other words, human connection) and will seek to satisfy these urges in unhealthy ways to mask their insecurities. In classrooms, students may present with behaviours such as seeking to appease or please in an attempt to keep others happy, alternatively they may refuse to engage as protection from painful feelings arising from a sense of inadequacy or fear of rejection. Negative attention is preferable to no attention for some students who can become adept at triggering unhealthy interaction with teachers and peers alike, unconsciously reinforcing disconnection and unbelonging in perpetual cycles. Particularly hard to reach students who struggle with belonging may need to spend time in safe spaces, building connections with support staff and other students. It is important for all community members to model and witness unconditional support and care being shown to such students because only then will wider perceptions begin to change. However, there is no place for being precious about systemically vulnerable students as it can provide opportunities for them to manipulate and control, making the job of other staff more difficult. It is beneficial for students to build relationships with all community members and for sustained efforts to optimise positive learning experiences when alternative arrangements are in place. Experience suggests that learning contributes significantly to students' wider sense of belonging in schools and students with additional needs working in exclusion rooms often struggle to complete work which is simply beyond their grasp without adaptations in place.

When students feel they belong in classrooms and schools, they are more confident to seek teachers out, state their preferences, ask for help, share their difficulties and take responsibility for mistakes. A special educational needs coordinator recently disclosed that on a learning walk observation day, some systemically vulnerable students experienced *no* adult interaction or connection throughout the entire day. Cultivating a sense of belonging – ensuring that regardless of aptitude, creed or disposition, every student feels worthy and loved in their school setting and actively connecting with them – is a key aspect of inclusive education which can change the course of a student's life.[9] I experienced this in a special school where despite the complex needs of the students who had all been excluded from mainstream schools, they flourished – self-esteem levels increasing from well-below to above-average in some cases,[10] achieving outstanding learning progress within the top 100 schools in the country and some reintegrating successfully into mainstream schools.

Try these (Appendix A: Belonging):

- Always put a smile on your face and make students feel welcome with a greeting every lesson, every day, especially those who experience a sense of difference or marginalisation.
- Check the intonation in your voice is naturally warm/friendly – tell students if you are having a bad day and apologise if your manner seems unwelcoming.
- Be aware of your facial expression in repose! Check it out and practice smiling through your eyes.
- Pretend to like students you, personally, find *difficult to like* – there will always be some because we all have insecurities that can be triggered by students at a subconscious level.
- Ask students if they have had a good weekend, day, lesson, break/lunch time as appropriate – show interest in them whether you are interested or not.
- Treat all students with the utmost courtesy and listen attentively to them *without starting to prepare a response in your mind*, regardless

of your preconceptions or possible misconceptions. This is more difficult than we think because most people listen with the intent to reply rather than understand.

- Talk to students about seating positions – some students have genuine reasons for wanting to sit away from or with particular students, so be curious; seek to find out more and be accommodating.
- *Never* take student attempts to reject you or their work personally, they are simply seeking to avoid painful feelings which we may not understand or connect with.
- Find reasons and ways to appreciate students for who they are, their differences and their struggles and model love and acceptance towards unpopular or uncool students whilst maintaining boundaries. This is powerful practice.

Notes

1 Allen K, Kern ML, Rozek CS, McInerney DM & Slavich GM (2021). 'Belonging: A Review of Conceptual Issues, An Integrative Framework, and Directions for Future Research', Taylor & Francis Online, https://doi.org/10.1080/00049530.2021.1883409.
2 Lieberman MD (2013). 'Social: Why Our Brains Are Wired to Connect', Oxford University Press.
3 Allen K, Kern ML, Rozek CS, McInerney DM & Slavich GM (2021). 'Belonging: A Review of Conceptual Issues, An Integrative Framework, and Directions for Future Research', Taylor & Francis Online, https://doi.org/10.1080/00049530.2021.1883409.
4 Brown B (2017). 'Braving the Wilderness: The Quest for True Belonging and the Courage to Stand Alone', Penguin Random House UK.
5 Brown B (2017). 'Braving the Wilderness: The Quest for True Belonging and the Courage to Stand Alone', Penguin Random House UK.
6 Brown B (2017). 'Braving the Wilderness: The Quest for True Belonging and the Courage to Stand Alone', Penguin Random House UK.
7 Brown B (2010). 'The Gifts of Imperfection: Let Go of Who You Think You're Supposed to Be and Embrace Who You Are', Penguin Random House UK.
8 Whitaker D (2021). 'The Kindness Principle: Making Relational Behaviour Management Work in Schools', Independent Thinking Press.
9 Brown B (2018). 'Dare to Lead: Brave Work. Tough Conversations. Whole Hearts', Penguin Random House UK.
10 Southampton Psychology Service (2003). 'Emotional Literacy Assessment and Intervention', GL Assessment Ltd.

3   Lessons on Learning and Trust

Students experience barriers to learning for a variety of reasons, but unless practitioners understand the interplay between *vulnerability, trust* and *learning*, their ability to reduce barriers and engage students will be compromised; as Aristotle contended, '[e]ducating the mind without educating the heart is no education at all'.[1] The concept of 'continual emotion-cognition interaction' points to emotions playing a critical role in the operations of mental processes, both in the 'simplest forms of exploration and learning as well as in higher-order cognition and sequences of organised behaviour'.[2] The next two sections provide a synopsis of vulnerability and relational trust which are foundational to understanding the impacts of teacher-student trust on learning.

Vulnerability

The notion of vulnerability has been used consistently in definitions of trust,[3] but understanding the concept was problematic prior to Brown's seminal research findings.[4] Irrespective of comfort or disadvantage, vulnerability is a *defining human characteristic* which is key to understanding a range of emotion-driven behaviours including relational trust and learning. At times of 'uncertainty, risk and emotional exposure',[4] humans are vulnerable, and although daily life is punctuated by such instances, typically people seek to push through the discomfort of difficult emotions without stopping to reflect. However, developing the capacity to be vulnerable through conscious emotional engagement is as important to relational health, as noticing and attending to pain in the body is to physical health.

The most common misconception about vulnerability is that it is *weakness*[5] and when posing the question to teachers in teacher training sessions, their responses demonstrated the veracity of this belief. The misconception of vulnerability as weakness has arguably contributed to the development of emotionally repressed cultures where emotional stoicism does not make people strong. In fact, most people 'were never

DOI: 10.4324/9781003466963-4

taught how to hold discomfort, sit with it, or communicate it' rather they learned how to discharge or suppress it.[6] Vulnerability is the seat of human emotion and while it is natural to be averse to painful feelings such as anxiety, disappointment or loss, vulnerability is also present in the most transformative moments of people's lives.[7] Consider for example, *love, innovation, creativity* or *change* – these are all processes suffused with risk, uncertainty or emotional exposure, but they are equally sources of human thriving.[8] Thus, if the capacity to bear emotional discomfort is compromised by the habitual use of defence mechanisms, the potential for life affirming emotions is also inadvertently compromised.[9] Although vulnerability is invariably hard to bear it is never weakness, rather it is an indication of *courage* as illustrated by the example of a hundred special force military personal who when questioned could not think of a single courageous act which did not require absolute vulnerability.[10]

Another misconception about vulnerability is that given optimum conditions or resourcefulness, people can eliminate vulnerability from their lives. However, this thinking aligns with *systemic* rather than human vulnerability, and it is especially important for educators to understand the distinction. *Systemic vulnerability* is a fundamental problem inherent in a range of system malfunctions such as biological, familial, structural, technological or economic. Educational barriers are typically attributable to systemic vulnerabilities such as special educational needs and disabilities (SEND), socio-economic factors, ethnicity, trauma, and so on, which place students at an obvious disadvantage. For decades, school staff have been tasked to minimise the impacts of vulnerability from student outcomes with insufficient distinction drawn between systemic and human vulnerability. It is perhaps unsurprising that educational inequity remains so problematic if the lens we are applying is distorted. Arguably, for practitioners, the term *vulnerability* has become synonymous with negative perceptions of disadvantage and educational failure which is unhealthy. There is an urgent need to reframe understanding and recognise that the remedy to *systemic* vulnerability in education will not arise from misconceptions of vulnerability as disadvantage or weakness. Whilst targeted system support is unquestionably needed, practitioners must endeavour to engage courageously with vulnerability themselves to help their students to learn and thrive. The following descriptors may be useful to avoid misleading messages:

- *Systemically* vulnerable is an accurate way to describe students with identified needs or disadvantages which impact on their access to education.
- Vulnerable describes a universal human characteristic. It is misleading to label some students as vulnerable because it conveys nothing more about them than is true for us all.

The impact of systemic factors on students' access to education can often be missed or misconstrued. For example, a large-scale, longitudinal research study in the US found that the number of words children were exposed to by age four differed by *38 million* between economically advantaged and disadvantaged families, thus significantly impacting their language development irrespective of cognitive ability. Moreover, further investigation revealed an *emotional deficit* when separating these words into categories of encouragement and discouragement.[11] Similarly, systemic vulnerability arising from ethnicity disadvantages a number of students and is a factor which is often overlooked.[12] It is questionable to what extent schools compound negative messages when systemically vulnerable students struggle with comprehension, structural discrimination or other difficulties and exhibit inappropriate behaviours to avoid or discharge vulnerability or shame. Brown's seminal research findings arguably warrant careful consideration[13,14,15,16]; for my part, a good track record in inclusive education had not led to understanding the significance of human vulnerability. I wrongly assumed that systemically vulnerable students were vulnerable, while I and others were not. Naturally, it is important to be alert to students who experience heightened levels of vulnerability as a result of systemic factors, but self-understanding of vulnerability is necessary to model healthy, reciprocal practice. As a student research participant adduced[17]:

> Some teachers don't get it, like they have to be powerful because they're a teacher but they don't … Teachers being vulnerable around students is powerful.

This quote adeptly illustrates the distinction between *invulnerability* leading to controlling, *power over* approaches and *empowering* others through authentic, vulnerable connection (see Chapters 6 and 12). As the adage goes, *we need to be the change we want to see* which necessitates developing the capacity to model healthy responses when experiencing emotional discomfort, and embracing vulnerability as the pathway to trust, learning and personal growth.

A few years ago, a child and adolescent specialist mental health practitioner asked me to attend family therapy sessions with a student, John, whose early childhood experiences had been exceptionally adverse and he was not making progress, either therapeutically or in school. Within the boundaries of one of the sessions, I risked sharing a personal experience from my childhood which felt emotionally exposing and uncomfortable. However, my action unlocked a door for John who finally found the courage to be vulnerable himself and disclose an equally emotionally exposing feeling which had been holding him back.

On our return to school, John was noticeably buoyant in mood. We talked about the session, and I commended him for his courage, relaying the quote ascribed to Joseph Campbell – 'the cave you fear to enter holds the treasures you seek'. After a moment's thought, with a smile on his face, he replied, 'And I love treasure!' John continued on his vulnerability journey and, against the odds, was able to complete his Year 11 exams in the mainstream school he had attended since Y7.

Although it is rare to be in situations where it is sagacious to share personally vulnerable experiences with students, on a daily basis, educators typically encounter a range of situations and interactions which trigger vulnerability. Teaching is an inherently vulnerable profession[18] involving relational risk and uncertainty on a daily basis, making vulnerability and trust important concepts for school staff to prioritise to avoid the pitfalls of invulnerability and distrust.

Trust – The Basics

Although trust is a frequently used word, understanding how it operates in relationships and its impact on learning is debatable. The starting point is to be clear that *vulnerability and trust are inseparable* because without risk or uncertainty, trust is a misnomer; relational trust requires relational vulnerability. Trusting action is 'choosing to risk making something you value vulnerable to another person's actions' or words.[19] What is valued can be both tangible and intangible; for example, a goal, idea, reputation, or sense of well-being can be vulnerable to others' actions. Conversely, distrust means that 'what is important to me is not safe with this person in this situation (or any situation)'.[20] Furthermore, trust is reciprocal in nature meaning that it develops over time through small moments of *reciprocal vulnerability* in relationships. In school environments, vulnerability can be particularly hard for students because of their status disparity with adults, so guarding against distrust is vital. Updated safeguarding guidance requires practitioners to maintain awareness of their *positionality* which is salient because *cultures most at risk of trust breakdown and misuse of power are those where hierarchical structures and status differentials are the norm*.[21] Unlike the medical profession which often generates high levels of professional trust, schools are prone to episodes of professional distrust which are hard to erase and can translate into generational distrust.

Understanding Learning

There is a critical relationship between trust and learning which came to light through focus group research with diverse groups of Year 8 male participants, both systemically vulnerable and not. Throughout the sessions, participants consistently identified learning as an inherently vulnerable process which entailed *the risk of making mistakes or sharing ideas; the fear of not understanding, of looking or feeling stupid; the anxiety of answering questions; and the uncertainty of teacher and peer reactions.*[22] These learning vulnerabilities are consistent with Holt's findings when working with primary students in the US in the late fifties where, even in the gentlest of schools:

> Students all said the same thing, that when the teacher asked them a question and they didn't know the answer, they were scared half to death. They said they were afraid of failing, afraid of being kept back, afraid of being called stupid, afraid of feeling themselves stupid.[23]

When asked how teachers gained and lost student trust, participants consistently described teacher behaviours that either minimised or exacerbated learning vulnerability. When students trusted their teachers they were willing to be vulnerable and take learning risks; when students distrusted their teachers, their willingness to engage in learning diminished. It was clear that learning was valued by all participants and that trusting or distrusting teachers either facilitated or became a barrier to their learning. In other words, *teacher-student trust is fundamental to learning because it operates as a conduit to mitigate the vulnerability of learning.* One participant described how he took notes in lessons of a teacher he distrusted, then tried to learn by himself at home which was not as effective. Another described how his response to a teacher breaking his trust was to put all his equipment away and stop working. Furthermore participants experienced a range of uncomfortable emotions as a result of teacher behaviours which diminished their trust including *anger, shame, isolation, upset, worry, sadness, confusion and humiliation.*[24] Equally significant however are participant findings pointing to the learning *benefits* trust can generate; teacher-student trust not only mitigates learning vulnerability but also promotes highly desirable *affective and cognitive aspects of learning*[25]:

- *Motivation*: 'You want to be in that lesson, you always try and contribute and work harder than you would usually'

- *Memory*: 'Lessons are easier to remember'
- *Concentration*: 'You pay attention more'
- *Confidence*: 'You just feel more secure with your knowledge and confident to risk sharing ideas'

As adults, it is vital to take the lead in creating environments that enable all students to feel sufficiently safe to be vulnerable, develop trust and learn. Systemically vulnerable students may not feel safe to be vulnerable for a range of reasons practitioners may be unaware of either historically or ongoing, but inclusion is at risk if worthy students are subconsciously perceived as those who can maintain positive relationships and participate appropriately in learning – although it is important to appreciate that trust matters a great deal to these students too:

> If you trust in the teacher, they trust us and we can trust them back but like if we don't feel we can trust them and they're not trusting us, I don't think there's a point. Children have to suffer for their education.[26]

Some of the most challenging students have underlying learning difficulties, frequently misunderstood or undiagnosed, which they go to extreme lengths to hide. This can be especially true for boys who are particularly reluctant to expose vulnerability in front of their peers or teachers and will avoid the risks at any cost if trust is lacking. On a daily basis, students *choose* or *refuse* to risk making their learning vulnerable to teachers' words or actions. Some students intentionally trigger sanctions and are prepared to miss out on lessons altogether if the risk of exposing learning-related vulnerability is too great. I have encountered numerous teachers who, at a loss with particular students, describe them as lazy, waste of space or perfectly capable; invariably, further investigation has revealed a learning difficulty which has been overlooked. Arguably, trust is a paradigm shifter which changes perceptions through the lens of vulnerability, promoting empathy, understanding and reciprocal learning, rather than judgement.

Cultivating Trust

As a multifaceted concept, trust requires attention to a range of affective and evaluative components; not only do students need to *feel* sufficiently safe to be vulnerable (affective components) but they also need to *evaluate* that teachers are trustworthy. In contrast to what people typically believe, trust is not some soft, abstract factor which can be left to chance, rather *trust is a realistic, actionable asset that people can generate*.[27] Having established the importance of teacher trust to student learning, the next step is to be informed about the approaches and actions that are aligned with cultivating it.

Affective Components

Care, connection and *empathy* are the key affective building blocks of trust which over time, alongside the practice of *trustworthy behaviours* (evaluative components), promote the willingness to risk making something of value (for students, their learning), vulnerable to teacher actions. Care, connection and empathy were prominent participant themes, compatible with the Finnish concept of *pedagogical love* which arose from the ideas of Martti Haavio, one of the most significant influencers in Finnish education. Pedagogical love extends to every learner regardless of ability, creed or disposition; it directs action and lays the foundation for motivation, creativity and perseverance in learners[28]; moreover, it is exemplified by reciprocal relationships of trust between all stakeholders and arguably foundational to Finland's educational success.

Pertinent to *care*, participants agreed that 'students are not bothered to learn when teachers don't care'. However, in the case of Mr Joseph, participants across all focus groups concurred that 'Out of all the teacher trusts they're not even half-way to Mr Joseph, Mr Joseph like really cared about us'. Conversely, another participant reflected 'I have seen [teachers] showing care, I think they know, but they still keep on doing the same things as before'.[29] It is salient that care is identified as the *only* element of trust that cannot be learned or developed if it is inherently lacking.[30] Care itself can feel vulnerable; there are emotional risks associated with caring, but experience suggests that when students say they don't care, they really do, more than is sometimes recognised.

Early on at a new school, I was asked to teach a GCSE Maths intervention group which included a disaffected Y10 student, Rose, who I had been told was unlikely to make it to the end of Y11. She was on a reduced timetable and had been walking out of Maths lessons since Year 8. She was prone to explosive outbursts and swearing at teachers. After persisting to chew gum in a way that could not be ignored in our first lesson, I gave her directed time out and followed up with her at the end of the lesson. When Rose told me she 'didn't care', I gave her my usual response – 'Well *I* care'. '*Why* do you care?' she challenged. It was a difficult question to answer, but I replied authentically and told her I didn't know why I cared; it was just something inside I was born with – it was probably why I became a teacher. In that moment, I think we both realised just how much *she* cared – about making it through school, passing her exams and her future. I realised too how scared Rose was to fail.

We discovered that in addition to other systemic vulnerabilities, Rose had dyslexic and dyscalculic characteristics. She began to attend extra support lessons willingly, gradually came back to school full time, benefited from teachers' understanding and took the initiative to support other students too. At the end of Y11, seeing Rose at her school Prom was a proud moment for her teachers. In August, I received a simple text message 'Miss, I passed!' Rose went on to an apprenticeship to become a special needs nursery practitioner; she had found the courage to be vulnerable and trust.

The second affective component of trust, *connection*, is another powerful change agent. *Sliding door* moments is a phrase coined by Gottman, an American psychologist and researcher,[31] to illustrate connecting moments of trust building in the following story:

Gottman was in bed one night and on the point of finishing an exciting mystery novel. However, he needed to use the bathroom and quickly got out of bed, intent on returning as soon as possible to continue reading. However, on his way back, he happened to notice his wife's face reflected in the mirror as she was brushing her hair, and she looked sad. All Gottman really wanted to do was to go back to bed and finish his book but instead, he chose to turn to his wife and find out why she was sad.

In schools, there are countless *sliding door* moments; in corridors, classrooms, dining halls and playgrounds, we have the same choice, to connect or turn away when we notice students in struggle. Practitioners need to be careful not to rely on establishing formal, academic connections at the expense of emotional bonds, and still expect students to engage with them.[32] Participants identified behaviours such as *noticing, listening, paying attention, acts of kindness, greeting students at the start of every lesson* and *never giving up on students* as connecting moments of trust building in schools.[33]

There is perhaps no greater exemplar of emotional connection than the third affective component of trust, *empathy* which is not only key to trust development but also an emotional literacy competence.

Empathy entails specific steps and practice and warrants a more detailed analysis which follows this chapter.

Trustworthiness (Evaluative Components)

Trustworthy characteristics have long been established by trust researchers as components of trust development.[34,35,36] Alongside affective components, individuals make conscious and subconscious evaluations about the trustworthiness of others based on a range of factors. Trustworthiness is a sensitive issue which needs to be approached with care because it concerns affective and ethical judgements about individuals that can set in motion 'benign and vicious circles' of distrust.[37] In order to avoid this pitfall, *school staff need to work collectively to operationalise the trustworthy components that matter most in school contexts by creating specific behaviour descriptors within identified categories which all members of the school community aim to model.* Only then will schools be in a position to have professional conversations with *actionable strategies* to address behaviours, rather than unwittingly inferring judgements about character.[38,39] Invariably, change *is* needed because whilst we all like to believe we are trustworthy, when we consider how many people we actually trust, the numbers rarely correspond.[40]

The characteristics of trustworthiness, illustrated in Figure 3.1, and explained further in the *Cultivating Trust* strategies section and signposted chapters are those which participants identified in the school context, although it is not intended to be a finite list: To facilitate memorisation, they are ordered using the acronym *ARISEN*:

- Accountability
- Reliability
- Integrity
- Support
- Emotional Safety
- Non-judgement

Pertinent to developing organisational trust, Brown[41] identifies two additional trustworthy characteristics arising from her research: Boundaries and another called the Vault. Arguably, both characteristics are important for practitioners in school organisations to be aware of and explanations are included in the *Cultivating Trust* strategies section.

Supportive staff environments are highly beneficial to developing trusting school cultures because there will inevitably be times when practitioners fall short, or feel let down by students, yet the impetus remains to be vulnerable and model trusting actions. However, if school

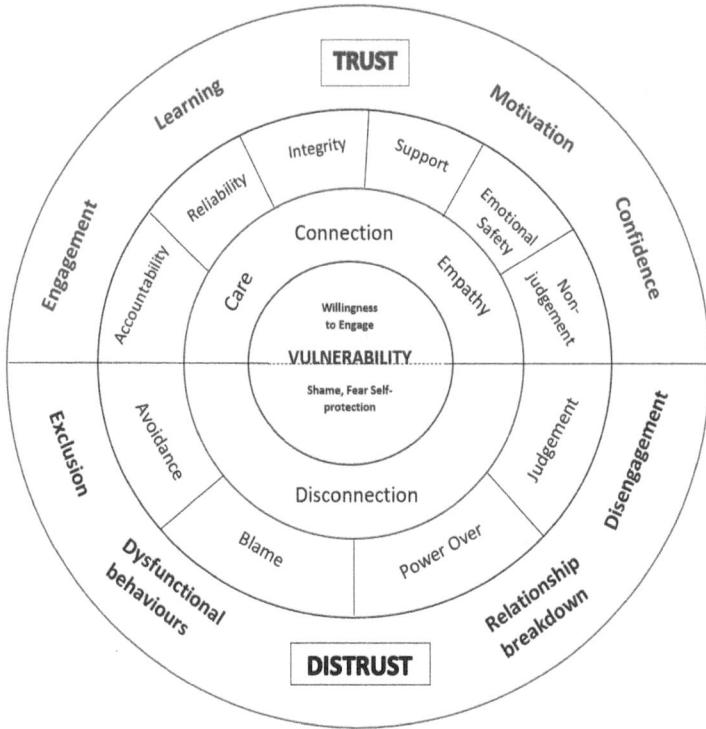

Figure 3.1 Thematic model linking key research findings on teacher-student trust.[42]

conditions are unfavourable, it is still possible to transform the learning climates in individual classrooms through trust practice.

> It's easier to learn when the teacher has trust because you know that if you don't understand, or like something you wouldn't expect happens, like all the different things that could happen, you always know that it will be OK because you have trust.[43]

Suggested Strategies: Learning Lessons (Appendix B)

Vulnerability – Try these:

- Be comfortable talking about feelings in lessons – they are a universal language. For example, as a greeting 'How are we all feeling today? Give some examples – happy, anxious, sad, etc. Or 'I'm feeling a bit…

today because…' Create feelings boards with students to use in tutor sessions to stimulate their emotional language and self-awareness.

- *Listen* with as much passion as you talk – aim for a 70% listening – 30% talking ratio. We connect emotionally when we listen intently, thoughtfully and silently. Listening helps us recognise vulnerable emotions which underlie behaviours.
- Use emotionally literate language and quietly give a name to the way a distressed student may be feeling. For example, 'I notice you seem angry, I notice you seem sad, I notice you seem worried. This will provide instant reassurance and provides *emotional holding* for the student.[44] Students are invariably quick to correct mistaken perceptions and communicate what they are actually feeling when we get it wrong.
- Be attuned to times when you feel *at risk, uncertain and emotionally exposed*. Practice identifying the underlying emotion and accepting the discomfort. Emotions do not come to stay, they come to pass. Give yourself and your students permission to feel vulnerable – it's human, normal and necessary.
- To learn more about vulnerability, take 20 minutes to watch 'The Power of Vulnerability'[45] which is amongst the five most viewed TED talks in the world. Alternatively read Professor Brene Brown's books on vulnerability and leadership.

Learning Strategies – Try these:

- Ensure all starter activities are mastery tasks, i.e. everyone can achieve them. Pay attention to your least able students and those who consistently find it difficult to settle. Repeat the favourites as often as you like. Predictability and routine work well at the start of every lesson.
- Speak simply and clearly, intentionally reduce the pace of your talk and ask for a volunteer to explain the task you have set. If s/he has difficulty explaining, repeat – clearer and simpler. This will facilitate understanding for students with a range of language difficulties.
- Impress on students that teachers are responsible for explaining things in a way they can understand, just as they are responsible for ensuring work is accessible for all students. Encourage a classroom climate in which speaking up is positively encouraged.
- Ensure students have access to written instructions or be prepared to repeat them as many times as necessary. Never assume students have not listened well – we do not know all the factors affecting their attention span and difficulties with attention and working memory are extremely frustrating for students too.
- Vulnerability and learning happen in the space between teachers and students, so reduce teacher talk to give students the time and

space they need to learn. Try recording a normal lesson and note the time you spend talking in relation to the time students spend learning.

- Reassure students repeatedly that mistakes are key to the process of learning and they are allowed to get things wrong. Tell them how you feel when you make mistakes and give examples of mistakes that have helped you learn.
- Tell students there are no stupid ideas or answers – it is a measure and mark of their courage that they are prepared to have a go and engage in the vulnerable process of learning. If student questions seem irrelevant, always demonstrate a curious approach – they may lack the language to ask the questions they need answers to.
- Present new material in small, achievable steps. The chunking technique is a commonly recommended strategy which helps all students to learn well, particularly those with language and processing difficulties.
- Provide scaffolding for students who refuse to work. Some students think 'If I don't try, I can't fail'. Be supportive, write the title, start the work, and see if they can risk just a little bit. Ask if they would like a peer to support them. If not, arrange to complete the work when you are able to give them individual support.
- Speak privately with students who consistently refuse to work to find out more about the problem. The message is, 'I will keep teaching you because I believe in you and I want you to achieve'. Tell me how I can support you better to … Would it help if I …?
- It is often helpful to give students a choice of task based on whether they are *feeling confident, need practice* or *are not quite there yet*. Developing the discipline of preparing lessons in this way becomes habitual and benefits all students.
- Present power points on cream backgrounds with a cursive, dark font and keep them as uncluttered as possible. Highlight or colour code key words or tasks. Provide an agenda for the lesson which students can refer to. This will benefit a range of student needs.
- Ask students to help you by scoring every lesson out of 10 for how well they think they have learnt in the lesson. It takes only seconds to write this down and is a helpful tool for reflection and reflexivity, both yours and theirs. Experience suggests students are generally very honest when asked to score their learning.

Cultivating Trustworthiness – Try these:

- **Accountability:** *Apologise to students* when you get it wrong and make amends. We all make mistakes, and saying sorry can feel vulnerable, especially if we've made a poor judgement call or feel our reputation is at stake. The benefits of apologising to students cannot be overstated in respect of building trust:

Teachers need to say sorry more to gain trust from students, so they can come to them when they need help or anything.[46]

It's important to realise when people are hurt and teachers have to realise when they've gone too far and say sorry. Teachers saying sorry makes the teacher and the student feel better.[47]

The accountability needed to build trust differs from professional, performance-related accountability which can be counter-productive to promoting reciprocal vulnerability practice if it entails judgement. When undergoing educational reform in the 1990s, it is noteworthy that Finland chose professional trust as an overarching aim, in contrast to the UK's aim of accountability.

- **Reliability:** *Carry out actions that you say you will.* At work, this necessitates staying aware of your strengths and weaknesses and not overpromising.[48] For participants, professional reliability was straightforward – it meant teachers *turning up, explaining clearly, ensuring work and homework are doable* (see Chapter 13) *and keeping order* (see Chapter 6 for more on keeping order).
- **Integrity:** *Practice your values* rather than simply professing them, displaying them or referring to school mission statements. Sometimes rather than acting in a way that is value-driven, we choose the easy option or avoid acting altogether. However, practicing values is essential to operationalising trust. Focus on *two key values* and *use them to guide your daily behaviours* towards others. For example, if a value you choose is trust, practise trust building strategies.
- **Support:** *Ask for the support you need* and be willing to *give unconditional support to others.* Help and support are important aspects of trustworthiness (see Chapter 10).
- **Emotional Safety:** Consistently practise *care, connection and empathy* and trust students by *giving them the benefit of the doubt.* There is often more to situations than meets the eye, and it is advantageous to remain neutral and follow up later, rather than to blame or accuse carelessly, especially in front of peers (see Chapter 6).
- **Non-judgement:** Refrain from making *moralistic* judgements about students; choose to believe they are *doing the best they can* and seek to understand the emotions underlying their behaviours. It is easy to assume people can do better, but this is more complex than we might think, raising questions about barriers to change and support needs (see Chapter 8).

- **Boundaries:** In contrast to *expectations* which communicate desires and wants that are often external and focused on the behaviour of others, boundaries reflect internal needs which are within people's control; they focus on the limits of acceptable behaviour. Boundary setting is important to well-being and ensures that clear messages are communicated about behaviours that are outside an individual's or organisational values.

  For example: 'I need you to respect this boundary (be explicit) because (state value/principle) is important. If you're unclear about what's okay or not okay, please ask'.

- **The Vault:** A safe container for other people's experiences or for information others choose to share.[49] The Vault protects people from breaches of confidentiality as well as idle gossip and is demonstrated by:

  - Keeping confidences
  - Not sharing information which is not the recipients to share

Notes

1 Aristotle (possibly falsely attributed), https://sententiaeantiquae.com/2017/05/27/head-and-heart-a-quotation-falsely-attributed-to-aristotle/. Accessed 26.03.25

2 Izard CE (2009, p. 18). 'Emotion Theory and Research: Highlights, Unanswered Questions, and Emerging Issues', *Annual Review of Psychology*, Vol. 60, pp. 1–25, https://www.annualreviews.org/docserver/fulltext/psych/60/1/annurev.psych.60.110707.163539.pdf?expires=1728467498&id=id&accname=guest&checksum=F6B6E4449A8AD744EA3AB9B86E7FCE81. Accessed 24.02.25.

3 Mayer RC, Davis JH, & Schoorman FD (1995). 'An Integrative Model of Organizational Trust', *The Academy of Management Review*, Vol. 20, No. 3, pp. 709–734.

4 Brown B (2018, p. 19). 'Dare to Lead: Brave Work. Tough Conversations. Whole Hearts', Penguin Random House UK.

5 Brown B (2018). 'Dare to Lead: Brave Work. Tough Conversations. Whole Hearts', Penguin Random House UK.

6 Brown B (2015, p. 51) 'Rising Strong: If We Are Brave Enough, Often Enough, We Will Fall', Penguin Random House UK.

7 Brown B (2018). 'Dare to Lead: Brave Work. Tough Conversations. Whole Hearts', Penguin Random House UK.

8 Brown B (2018). 'Dare to Lead: Brave Work. Tough Conversations. Whole Hearts', Penguin Random House UK.

9 Brown B (2018). 'Dare to Lead: Brave Work. Tough Conversations. Whole Hearts', Penguin Random House UK.

10 Brown B (2017). 'Braving the Wilderness: The Quest for True Belonging and the Courage to Stand Alone', Penguin Random House UK.

11 Jones J (2009). 'The Magic-Weaving Business: Finding the Heart of Learning and Teaching', Leannta Publishing.

12 The Secretary of State for Education (2019). 'The Timpson Review of School Exclusion', https://assets.publishing.service.gov.uk/government/uploads/system/uploads/attachment_data/file/807862/Timpson_review.pdf. Accessed 11.06.21.

13 Brown B (2012). 'Daring Greatly: How the Courage to be Vulnerable Transform the Way We Live, Love, Parent and Lead', Penguin Random House UK.
14 Brown B (2015). 'Rising Strong: If We Are Brave Enough, Often Enough, We Will Fall', Vermillion, Penguin Random House UK.
15 Brown B (2017). 'Braving the Wilderness: The Quest for True Belonging and the Courage to Stand Alone', Penguin Random House UK.
16 Brown B (2018). 'Dare to Lead: Brave Work. Tough Conversations. Whole Hearts', Penguin Random House UK.
17 Byrnell VH (2019, Appendix M, p. 5). 'Academic Paper and Conference Presentation', St Mary's University.
18 Kelchtermans G (2009). 'Who I Am in How I Teach Is the Message: Self-Understanding, Vulnerability and Reflection', *Teachers and Teaching: Theory and Practice*, Vol. 15, No. 2, pp. 257–272.
19 Feltman C (2009, p. 9). 'The Thin Book of Trust: An Essential Primer for Building Trust at Work', Thin Book Publishing Co.
20 Feltman C (2009, p. 8). 'The Thin Book of Trust: An Essential Primer for Building Trust at Work', Thin Book Publishing Co.
21 Brown B (2018). 'Dare to Lead: Brave Work. Tough Conversations. Whole Hearts', Penguin Random House UK.
22 Byrnell VH (2019). 'Academic Paper and Conference Presentation', St Mary's University.
23 Holt J (1982, p. 71). 'How Children Fail', Revised Edition, Perseus Books.
24 Byrnell VH (2019). 'Academic Paper and Conference Presentation', St Mary's University.
25 Byrnell VH (2019, Appendix M, p. 1). 'Academic Paper and Conference Presentation', St Mary's University.
26 Byrnell VH (2019, Appendix M, p. 3). 'Academic Paper and Conference Presentation', St Mary's University.
27 Covey MR & Merrill RR (2008). 'The Speed of Trust: The One Thing That Changes Everything', Reprint edition, Free Press.
28 Maatta K & Uusiautti S (2013). 'Pedagogical Love and Good Teacherhood', *Education*, Vol. 17, No. 2, https://doi.org/10.37119/ojs2011.v17i2.81.
29 Byrnell VH (2019, Appendix M, p. 1). 'Academic Paper and Conference Presentation', St Mary's University.
30 Brown B (2018). 'Dare to Lead: Brave Work. Tough Conversations. Whole Hearts', Penguin Random House UK.
31 John G (referencing the 1998 Gwyneth Paltrow film "Sliding Doors") (2011). 'How to Build Trust', Greater Good Science Centre, https://www.youtube.com/watch?v=rgWnadSi91s. Accessed 24.02.25.
32 Whittaker D (2021). 'The Kindness Principle: Making Relational Behaviour Management Work in Schools', Independent Thinking Press.
33 Byrnell VH (2019). 'Academic Paper and Conference Presentation', St Mary's University.
34 Mayer RC, Davis JH & Schoorman FD (1995). 'An Integrative Model of Organizational Trust', *The Academy of Management Review*, Vol. 20, No. 3, pp. 709–734.
35 Adams CM (2013). 'Collective Trust: A Social Indicator of Instructional Capacity', *Journal of Educational Administration*, Vol. 51, No. 3, pp. 363–382, https://doi.org/10.1108/09578231311311519.
36 Heyns M & Rothmann S (2015). 'Dimensionality of Trust: An Analysis of the Relations Between Propensity, Trustworthiness and Trust', *SA Journal of Industrial Psychology*, Vol. 41, pp. 1–12.

37 Bottery M (2012, p. 4). 'Trust: its importance for educators', *Management in Education*, Vol. 18, No. 5, https://doi.org/10.1177/089202060501800502?download=true&journalCode=mie.
38 Feltman C (2009). 'The Thin Book of Trust: An Essential Primer for Building Trust at Work', Thin Book Publishing Co.
39 Brown B (2012, p. 224). 'Daring Greatly: How the Courage to be Vulnerable Transform the Way We Live, Love, Parent and Lead', Penguin Random House UK.
40 Brown B (2018). 'Dare to Lead: Brave Work. Tough Conversations. Whole Hearts', Penguin Random House UK.
41 Brown B (2015). 'Rising Strong: If We Are Brave Enough, Often Enough, We Will Fall', Vermillion, Penguin Random House UK.
42 Byrnell VH (2019). 'Academic Paper and Conference Presentation', St Mary's University.
43 Byrnell VH (2019, Appendix M, p. 3). 'Academic Paper and Conference Presentation', St Mary's University.
44 Greenhalgh P (1994). 'Emotional Growth and Learning', Routledge.
45 Brown B (2010). 'The Power of Vulnerability', TEDxHouston, https://www.youtube.com/watch?v=iCvmsMzlF7o. Accessed 24.02.25.
46 Byrnell VH (2019, Appendix M, p. 5). 'Academic Paper and Conference Presentation', St Mary's University.
47 Byrnell VH (2019, Appendix M, p. 5). 'Academic Paper and Conference Presentation', St Mary's University.
48 Brown B (2018). 'Dare to Lead: Brave Work. Tough Conversations. Whole Hearts', Penguin Random House UK.
49 Brown B (2015, p. 199). 'Rising Strong: If We Are Brave Enough, Often Enough, We Will Fall', Vermillion, Penguin Random House UK.

4 Empathy Hits and Misses

In the early 2000s, emotional literacy or intelligence (EL) was promoted as an educational competence by the government in office as a result of studies pointing to positive links with self-esteem and life outcomes. Although the Social & Emotional Aspects of Learning curriculum was archived in 2011,[1] the use of emotional literacy assessments such as those developed by Southampton Psychology Service[2] remains a valuable resource to identify emotionally vulnerable students, including those who are quiet or withdrawn and easily overlooked (see Appendix L). EL was established by Daniel Coleman[3] to comprise five competences: *self-awareness, self-regulation, motivation, empathy,* and *social skills.* Given the importance of empathy to trust development, it is the focus of this chapter which begins with an overview of four teachable attributes drawn from seminal empathy research by a nursing scholar, Teresa Wiseman.[4]

Take the Perspective of Others

Perspective-taking requires conscious intent because adults are more likely to view the perspective of others through the lens of their own beliefs and experiences if they have not developed the skill in childhood. Young people on the other hand are generally more receptive to perspective-taking because of a natural curiosity about the world and how others operate in it.[5] The first step towards empathy is to try and understand the student perspective which often differs from the adult assumption. To achieve genuine understanding, adults need to let go of being the knower, listen carefully and become the learner. *'Tell me more"* or *"tell me how this is for you, what are you thinking?'* are responses which help to develop and align with perspective-taking.

Stay Out of Judgement

Empathy requires listening *non-judgementally* which means there is no *right or wrong* – no *moral judgement* when practicing empathy. People are most likely to judge others in areas where they themselves are

DOI: 10.4324/9781003466963-5

susceptible to feelings of low self-worth or shame, so judgement can become an unhealthy cycle.[6] Again curiosity, active listening and becoming a learner are necessary to stay out of judgement. The Six Blind Men and the Elephant fable is an effective resource which is widely available online to illustrate non-judgemental perspective-taking.[7] I have recounted the story many times to students who noticeably feel more relaxed when they realise their perspective is not being viewed as deficient or wrong which in turn facilitates productive discussion.

Connect with Others' Emotions

A sufficient level of emotional self-awareness is a *prerequisite* for empathy because it is only possible to *connect* with the way someone else is feeling if people recognise the feeling in themselves. Emotionally literate people are able to read feeling messages others communicate through a range of non-verbal channels.[8] Empathy is a vulnerable choice because it requires personally connecting with another's feeling by unlocking that feeling in ourselves.[9] Self-awareness can be a limiting factor for students with low EL levels, but self-awareness like perspective-taking, can be developed. Actively practicing connection with students' emotions is highly pertinent to trust development as it enables a shift in focus to curiosity and understanding rather than reacting to behaviours in a way that risks distrust.

Communicate Understanding of Others' Emotions

Lastly it is crucial to be aware of the barriers to empathy – the empathy misses, when communicating understanding of others' emotions. *Sympathising, reassuring, minimising the problem, giving advice, downplaying the situation* or *over sharing personal experiences* are all common, well-intentioned approaches that completely miss empathetic connection.[10,11] It is easy to get empathy wrong as I have experienced, without learning the steps, knowing the barriers and practising it. Simple responses such as 'Me too' or 'I get it' are examples of responses that work well to communicate empathetic understanding but only if the choice to connect with the feeling has been actioned. Students are adept at sensing insincerity in adults, and students are often highly perceptive and attuned to adults' emotional responses.

Learning the skills to practice empathetic connection is only part of the picture however, the ability to extend empathy to others also correlates with the level of self-compassion people extend to themselves.[12] This corresponding need for *self*-compassion points to the importance of monitoring *self-talk* carefully, especially when feeling vulnerable or confronted with the realisation of mistakes or failures. The aim is to treat and speak to *ourselves,* and encourage students to treat and speak to themselves, with as much kindness as we would treat a good friend because 'if your compassion does not include *yourself,* it is incomplete'.[13] A consequence of lacking self-compassion is that it is less likely there will be sufficient compassion in the reserves to draw from to extend to others. Emotional practice requires mental energy and thus it is also pertinent that empathy is one of the first competencies people tend to lose when they are overtired or stressed.

Inclusive Behaviour Management

Tensions between traditional and inclusive behaviour management approaches are inevitable because the manner in which sanctions are typically issued bypasses empathy and communicates judgement. Moreover behaviourist techniques used to emphasise reinforcement and punishment rarely succeed in long-term behavioural change for systemically vulnerable students[14] (see also Chapter 13). There is ample evidence to suggest that traditional sanction systems rarely achieve behaviour *change* in students most at risk of exclusion because they tend to reinforce negative self-perception and failure rather than promoting a sense of responsibility for unacceptable behaviours.[15] Significantly, Neff's[16] findings point to empathetic responses being unquestionably more motivating in respect of personal change than admonishment. Relapses in behaviour are important learning events, but they are often the stage when we give up with troubled students on the basis that they have had so much help and still can't get it right.[17] Getting it wrong and making mistakes feels vulnerable, and for systemically vulnerable students it can often trigger shame. However, when met with empathetic responses, students are more likely to de-escalate their behaviours and engage. Conversely, judgement and use of power over approaches lead to disconnection and fear 'fuelling anxiety in even the most well-behaved children'[18] as the following case study illustrates.

A colleague, Mr Jones, regularly used zero tolerance approaches in lessons which led to shouting loudly and angrily at students for minor misdemeanours. I happened to be in Mr Jones's lesson when a student started to whisper to a peer. As Mr Jones noticed and turned towards them, another student, Sam, immediately burst into tears and walked out. I went out and spoke with Sam who requested to complete his work outside the classroom for the remainder of the lesson. At the end of the lesson, I spoke with Mr

Jones who was concerned because Sam was a high-achieving student whose behaviour was always exemplary. I explained that Sam had a problem with the shouting. 'But I hadn't shouted', Mr Jones answered, perplexed. 'No, but the anxiety that you were about to shout was sufficient to cause him to feel afraid and upset', I replied. All credit to Mr Jones who subsequently changed his practice and began to connect more sensitively with all his students.

There has been an increasing shift towards 'zero tolerance' approaches in behaviour management policy, and whilst some practitioners may be successful in counterbalancing the impact, experience points to the need for *flexible* rather than rigid approaches to achieve inclusivity and build trust. Flexible approaches require discretion; they are vulnerable and can be a source of contention for staff, prompting concerns about inconsistency and perceptions of unfairness. However, when students complain about favourable treatment towards others, my experiences invariably point to an unmet need of their own which is revealed through further discussion. Students are well aware of their peers' needs and difficulties, and modelling discretion and empathy has time and again proved beneficial to inclusive practice. Zero-tolerance approaches risk exacerbating a disproven belief in the power of fear to motivate compounding barriers to student learning. As Edmonson explains:

> Research in neuroscience shows that fear consumes physiologic resources, diverting them from parts of the brain that manage working memory and process new information. This impairs analytic thinking, creative insight, and problem solving ... Hierarchy (or, more specifically, the fear it creates when not handled well) reduces psychological safety.[19]

Rethinking approaches to school sanction systems does not in any way diminish the need for clear boundaries, personal responsibility and sanctions for dangerous or anti-social behaviours. Neither does it preclude strong, planned responses which are necessary to address specific situations; schools, after all, need to prepare students for the reality of life. However, it does mean that practitioners need to reflect carefully on their approach to young people when they get things wrong, repeat mistakes or seem slow to learn. All too often time and energy are spent dealing with a spiral of behaviour concerns resulting from responses which perpetuate relational breakdown and disconnection. Practicing empathetic connection is a trust-building response which leads to empowerment; not only are students more likely to share their difficulties, apologise and accept sanctions, but teachers too will gain understanding about the support students need to put things right. All too often students desperately need support to make amends and take responsibility – sometimes they have few role models to learn from and the aim is to develop sufficient trust to allow teachers to be theirs. Supporting students to learn these lessons requires consistent emotional responses aligned with trust building. A recent research study investigating critical classroom practice for building teacher-student trust points to *flexibility*, *kindness*, *patience* and *forgiveness* signalling that teachers genuinely understand students' challenges and can be 'counted on to help them along the way'.[20]

Try These (Appendix C: Empathy and Inclusive Behaviour Management)

- Learn the empathy attributes and practice them. Pay attention to whether you are connecting emotionally with others' feelings or expressing sympathy or reassurance. Avoid over-sharing personal experiences, downplaying the situation or giving advice.
- Practise self-compassion and monitor your self-talk carefully. If you notice you are berating yourself, try and reframe your inner conversation. Realise you did the best you could at the time and use the experience for learning.
- Praise *desired* student behaviours *first*. It is easy to be distracted by unwanted behaviours but praise first sends a powerful message of connection to students.
- Use eye contact and non-verbal gestures wherever possible to support behaviour requests. For example, flat hand being lowered (sit down), hand to ear (listening), finger to mouth (quiet please), revolving finger (turn around), hand to head (think), show five digits, mime *take 5*, then point to door (take time out).
- Avoid using negative or confrontational language. Clearly and simply state the desired behaviour, ending with a thank you. This communicates that you anticipate cooperation and expect the best. For example, 'Aaron, sitting quietly in your seat now, thank you. Sophie, paying attention and listening now, thank you. Theo, break time's over, back to work mode now, thank you'.
- Try using (although not overusing) the phrase 'I'm choosing to ignore …' to avoid confrontation. Emotionally aroused students are often looking for an outlet so don't give them one. For example, 'I'm choosing to ignore your rudeness' sends a clear, public message that the student has overstepped a boundary *but you will address it when you are ready to do so*. Continue the lesson. If the behaviour

continues, you could try it once more, for example, 'I'm still choosing to ignore your rudeness, have you made a start yet?' If they put it right great, if not set an activity and *quietly* speak to the student. Use emotionally literate language. 'I notice you seem angry, but the rudeness is unacceptable. Do you need support, is everything OK?' If the student remains unresponsive and unable to learn in class, they may need time out. This is not failure; it is noticing, connection, upholding boundaries, support and trust building. You can follow up at a suitable time.

- *Give take up time* and *walk away* if a student point blank refuses to respond to a request. It is one of the most challenging behaviours to be confronted with and triggers huge vulnerability in teachers; but remember, the student is emotionally stuck. It is not a challenge to your personal authority and if appropriate *you can decide to change your mind*. For example, 'Actually I think it's best you stay there Sarah, Lauren would you mind moving instead?' Or 'Perhaps you need some thinking time? I'll come back to you in a few minutes'. These types of responses are good examples of teachers modelling vulnerability well. The outcome is uncertain – notice and accept the vulnerability.

- Find opportunities to tell students that they are kind/considerate/ polite, they are hardworking/talented/funny, they make you feel proud/happy. Whether you believe it or not, their self-perceptions will begin to change. A colleague of mine recounted how she would tell a challenging student in her tutor group Zara, that she was 'the sunshine in her life'. When she subsequently told another sad, systemically vulnerable student that he was her favourite, he replied that he knew he wasn't because Zara was her sunshine. She replied 'And you are the moonlight'. The student beamed.

- Praise all positive social interaction that you observe. Be explicit, for example, 'You are listening really well to Jordan's point of view', 'that's kind of you to let Kamil go first', 'you are a good friend to support Cameron'.

- Praise students for the courage to be honest but don't expect truth, loyalty or respect as a matter of course. These attributes are only likely to be demonstrated by students who feel secure and loved. Students live out their experiences and honesty, loyalty and respect may only be gained when trust is established.

- If sanctions are necessary, communicate *quietly and privately* with the student. Avoid making sanctions public and if the student him/ herself chooses to do so in an attempt to gain attention, you can simply walk away and say 'end of conversation'.

- Give students responsibilities, ask for their help and allow them access to trips and positive experiences. Be wary of linking responsibilities and positive experiences to rewards; the benefits to self-esteem and trust building are invaluable.

Notes

1 DFE (2005). 'Social and Emotional Aspects of Learning (SEAL): Improving Behaviour, Improving Learning', The National Strategies, archived on 12 August 2011.
2 Southampton Psychology Service (2003). 'Emotional Literacy Assessment and Intervention', Edited by Adrian Faupel, GL Assessment Ltd.
3 Coleman D (1996). 'Emotional Intelligence: Why It Can Matter More Than IQ', Bloomsbury Publishing Plc.
4 Wiseman T (1996). 'A Concept Analysis of Empathy', *Journal of Advanced Nursing*, Vol. 23, pp. 1162–1167, https://doi.org/10.1046/j.1365-2648.1996.12213.x.
5 Brown B (2018). 'Dare to Lead: Brave Work. Tough Conversations. Whole Hearts', Penguin Random House UK.
6 Brown B (2018). 'Dare to Lead: Brave Work. Tough Conversations. Whole Hearts', Penguin Random House UK.
7 Saxe JG (1872). 'The Blind Men and the Elephant', https://en.wikisource.org/wiki/The_poems_of_John_Godfrey_Saxe/The_Blind_Men_and_the_Elephant. Accessed 24.02.25.
8 Southampton Psychology Service (2003). 'Emotional Literacy Assessment and Intervention', Edited by Adrian Faupel, GL Assessment Ltd.
9 Brown B (2018). 'Dare to Lead: Brave Work. Tough Conversations. Whole Hearts', Penguin Random House UK.
10 Rosenberg MB (2003). 'Non Violent Communication: A Language of Life', 2nd Edition, PuddleDancer Press.
11 Brown B (2018). 'Dare to Lead: Brave Work. Tough Conversations. Whole Hearts', Penguin Random House UK.
12 Neff K (2011). 'Self-Compassion: The Proven Power of Being Kind to Yourself', William Morrow.
13 Kornfield J (1994). 'Buddha's Little Instruction Book', Bantam Books.
14 Whitaker D (2021). 'The Kindness Principle: Making Relational Behaviour Management Work in Schools', Independent Thinking Press.
15 Whittaker D (2021). 'The Kindness Principle: Making Relational Behaviour Management Work in Schools', Independent Thinking Press.
16 Neff K (2011). 'Self-Compassion: The Proven Power of Being Kind to Yourself', William Morrow.
17 Delaney M (2009). 'Teaching the Unteachable: Practical Ideas to Give Teachers Hope and Help When Behaviour Management Strategies Fail', Worth Publishing Ltd.
18 Whittaker D (2021, p. 22). 'The Kindness Principle: Making Relational Behaviour Management Work in Schools', Independent Thinking Press.
19 Edmondson AC (2019, p. 14). 'The Fearless Organisation: Creating Psychological Safety in the Workplace for Learning, Innovation, and Growth', John Wiley & Sons, Inc.
20 Brake A (2019, p. 287). 'Right from the Start: Critical Classroom Practices for Building Teacher-Student Trust in the First 10 Weeks of Ninth Grade', *The Urban Review*, Vol. 52, pp. 277–298, https://doi.org/10.1007/s11256-019-00528-z.

5   Shame Talk

Significant developments in shame research over the past 15 years point to shame as a major contributor to *poor mental health, addiction, unethical behaviour, violence, aggression,* and *bullying*[1] and thus the emotional root of significant levels of human dysfunction. The power of shame resides in its unspeakability, so the longer people avoid talking about shame – its drivers, the way it operates and how to combat it – the more emotionally compromised the human race becomes. Schools are by no means exempt from shame which can inhibit the courage to be vulnerable, trust and learn. Thus, it is time to start speaking about shame and to educate school communities, both practitioners and students alike. As Brown attests, shame may be tough to talk about but 'the conversation isn't nearly as dangerous as what we're creating with our silence'.[2]

It is helpful to begin with three shame basics[3]:

1   Everyone experiences shame (bar sociopaths).
2   Everyone is afraid to talk about shame.
3   The less people talk about shame, the more power it has over their lives.

Shame is defined as 'the intensely painful feeling or experience of believing that we are flawed and therefore unworthy of love, belonging and connection'.[4] As previously indicated, belonging and connection are genetically embedded human needs so a deep-seated fear of *disconnection* renders people unable to be vulnerable for fear of rejection or judgement by others.[5] It is often the case that when people struggle with vulnerability they are adept in matters of shame, but the problem is that shame is a corrosive emotion which depletes the capacity for human belonging. A simple starting point for shame conversations is to differentiate shame from *humiliation, guilt* and *embarrassment* as these emotions are commonly conflated. Although humiliation can

DOI: 10.4324/9781003466963-6

feel similar to shame, when experiencing humiliation people typically have a sense of not deserving the behaviour directed at them[6]; when feeling humiliated, a sense of anger or outrage can be a *healthy* response. On the other hand, guilt and embarrassment have different foci; although guilt is uncomfortable, the focus is on a *behaviour* that is regretted and when followed by an apology and making amends it can be helpful in motivating meaningful change.[7] Embarrassment is typically accompanied by the recognition of a commonly experienced feeling which people are generally willing to share. In contrast, shame is believing *oneself* to be inherently flawed and deserving of the shame experienced.

As indicated, shame derives its power from remaining unspoken and hidden and can be experienced as such a negative, intense emotion of self-loathing that it can lead people to disown or discharge it in destructive ways.[8] Shame can remain concealed for years, especially for children who have been victims of aggression or abuse. I have encountered two cases of students shamed in childhood who developed the ability to disassociate themselves from their actions to the extent that they believed the lies they told and connection with others remained a constant struggle. Adverse childhood experiences leading to low self-worth can result in *shame proneness* for some people who live with the belief that they themselves are bad and unlovable. It is also useful to recognise that the responses of shame prone individuals in the present are shaped by emotional memories of when shame was previously experienced.[9] On one occasion, a student in a class I was teaching was called "stupid" by a peer, and his immediate reaction was to launch into aggressive, attack mode. It transpired the student had been called stupid repeatedly by his father from an early age and even slapped on the face as a consequence. Trauma, abuse, poverty and bullying are all shame-inducing experiences, the casualties of which are invulnerability, loss of connection and low self-worth.

A study on shame led by a team of scientists with more than 2,600 volunteers in Bern University, Switzerland, found that *adolescents are the most prone age group to feelings of shame* because the identities of teenagers are not completely formed.[10] Furthermore, young people 'are expected to conform to all manner of norms that define their place in school and society and uncertainty about how to deal with these external expectations may make them quicker to feel shame'.[11] Gender also plays a part, both in the way shame manifests and its triggers, which have been found to vary between females and males.[12,13] Identifying shame and understanding its triggers is a helpful starting point for developing shame resilience, and Brown's research identifies the following gendered and general categories[14]:

Female shame:

Imperfection
Never good enough; not attractive enough, not cool enough, not thin
   enough ...
Exposing hidden flaws
Motherhood
Maternal judgment

Male shame:

Weakness
Failure
Being wrong
A sense of being defective
Showing fear, being criticised or ridiculed
Fatherhood
Paternal judgement

General categories:

Appearance and body image
Aging
Money and work
Family
Parenting
Mental and physical health
Surviving trauma
Being stereotyped or labelled
Religion

A conversation with a Maths teacher about gender-related shame triggers was a revelatory moment that made sense of her recent experience, teaching a Maths investigation lesson to separate boys and girls classes. In both lessons, the teacher had begun by emphasising that there were *no wrong answers*, and the boys had engaged enthusiastically in the lesson. Feeling confident, the teacher taught the same lesson to the girls' class who hated it; the girls wanted answers that could be *perfectly right*, whereas the boys were far more comfortable feeling they *couldn't be wrong*. Perfectionism in ourselves and students is a trait we need to be alert to because perfectionism is not about aiming high or healthy achievement and growth; perfectionism is rooted in the fear of not meeting expectations or falling short – it is a defence mechanism to minimise or avoid the pain of shame-inducing judgement, criticism or blame.[15] It is also significant that there are strong similarities between the *learning vulnerabilities* identified by the male participants and *male shame triggers* (being wrong, failing, a sense of being defective) which raises important questions about gender imbalance in school exclusion and pupil referral units. Whilst it may not be possible to achieve inclusion for all students in mainstream schools because of the complexity of their needs, for many students, negative experiences of school and inclusion are exacerbated following transition to secondary school. As curriculum expectations increase and identity is fragile, the risks of learning-related shame are heightened.

Unhealthy shame responses are common in both adult and student populations, and shame is invariably present in school organisations. Sometimes, it can be readily identified, for example, in the case of a teacher belittling a student; however, less obvious signs include behaviours such as *gossip, blame, criticism, judgement, favouritism, comparison, discrimination, perfectionism, teasing, cover-ups* or *abuse of power*.[16] If left unchecked, shame can remain concealed in organisations where it operates as an invisible enemy, sabotaging cultural and relational health. Students who bully and tease in response to hidden shame can easily figure out what makes others feel ashamed, and they are highly skilled at triggering shame in their peers which makes shame a contagious emotion.[17] Across the UK, 35% of pupils reported being bullied in a way that made them feel frightened or upset from statistics gathered between 2014 and 2018; furthermore, in 2019, a poll carried out for the Anti-Bullying Alliance found that 11% of surveyed children said they missed school due to bullying.[18] Also salient is a survey carried out by the NASUWT in 2019 which reported that four out of every five teachers said they had experienced bullying at work;[19] such data clearly indicates the importance of taking shame issues seriously, demystifying and engaging in shame talk.

There are three common shame defences to look out for,[20,21] although in practice, it is likely that people use all three at different times.[22] Practitioners would benefit from having regular conversations with colleagues to identify shame-prone students because when using these defences, students will struggle to connect, learn or talk about what is happening.

Moving Against: trying to gain power and control over others using aggression
Moving Away: withdrawing, hiding, keeping silent and keeping secrets
Moving Toward: seeking to please and appease

A few years ago, I was asked to talk with Billy who was overheard making an unprovoked, serious threat to kill a peer. He categorically denied making the threat and continued to protest his innocence, preventing resolution. Eventually, after reassuring Billy that I knew him to be a naturally kind and gentle boy, he made up a story to explain why his peer would say he had made this threat; it was fabrication, and I began to sense frustration and failure.

However, I recognised the use of two shame defences – moving against (the threat to kill) and moving toward (seeking to appease me). Connecting with Billy's shame, I dug deep and began a conversation which felt vulnerable. I shared that we all feel shame, and it makes us feel alone and scared – especially when we're afraid of getting into trouble. Tears started rolling down Billy's face, and he began to sob. Falteringly, between sobs, he began to share that he had been fighting with his younger brother the previous night, and his mother had been taken to hospital with heart problems.

It transpired Billy had been repeatedly *blamed* for increasing his mother's stress levels, and he believed her mental illness and heart problem were his fault; she was going to die, and he was a bad child. This was the shame Billy had carried with him to school that morning, and being too painful for him to bear, he had sought to discharge it. Speaking his shame enabled resolution and the school to seek further protection measures for Billy.

The good news is that developing shame resilience is possible. Navigating the experience of shame 'without sacrificing our values' and coming out the other side 'with more courage, compassion, and connection than we had going into it' is ultimately about moving from shame to empathy, which involves several elements.[23]

- Initial recognition and understanding of shame, both the messages or experiences which triggered it and the physical symptoms that accompany it.
- The ability to self-calm the limbic system until the prefrontal cortex, which operates more slowly, enables rational thought. Developments in neuroscience suggest shame can be experienced as actual physical pain or discomfort (think of students with repeating, seemingly spurious aches, pains and ailments), so calming the limbic system may sometimes require strategies for tolerating physical pain.

- Sufficient levels of self-compassion as well as the willingness to reach out, own and share the story with a trusted individual.

Empathetic connection enables people to share the experience of a painful human feeling, so they no longer feel alone, they are worthy and lovable regardless of undesirable character traits which all humans have; ultimately, it is the part of ourselves we 'choose to act on' which matters most.[24] Furthermore, in shame-resilient cultures, self-worth is not centred on what people produce or achieve but on *who* people are. In schools, it is the adults who will invariably need to recognise when their students are in shame and reach out to them. To remain engaged, connected and learning, students need to be vulnerable, and although teachers' time is limited in class, paying attention and identifying students who adopt shame defences enable proactive steps towards empathetic connection, learning and trust.

Try These (Appendix D: Shame Talk)

- *Learn* the defensive responses to shame and identify students who regularly use shame shields. This will be the first step to understanding more about their shame triggers.
- Start a conversation with colleagues or your department about shame and its impact on student behaviours and learning. Collaboratively identify students who regularly use shame shields to increase awareness and consistency of practitioner responses.
- *Practise* the empathy attributes outlined in Chapter 3 – students will not judge you for getting it wrong and you will begin to identify empathy hits and misses by their responses. The aim is to connect with their feelings to alleviate feelings of isolation. Encourage them to be kind to themselves.
- Recognise and accept that developing trust with highly shame-prone students will take time and support. Sometimes, it will require referral to therapeutic specialists if shame is embedded from adverse childhood experiences. Experience suggests one of the greatest casualties of the austerity years is a reduction in well-being and counselling services in schools. However, we must continue to press for appropriate provision where it is most needed.
- If you suspect students are immobilised by shame, aim to give them time, space and kindness.
- If you experience a student using the 'Moving Against' shield and empathetic approaches fail, the student will invariably need time out in a safe space. Shame-induced anger is an intense fear response – the fear of disconnection or possibly a relived shame experience from the past. In this state, students are compromised in their ability to

self-regulate, and recognising this is helpful for you and the student. Remaining calm, decisive and confident at such times will provide safety for you and others.

- Recommended reading: Brene Brown (2012) 'Daring Greatly: How the Courage to be Vulnerable Transforms the Way We Live, Love, Parent and Lead (Chapter 3)', Understanding and Combating Shame, Penguin Random House UK.

Notes

1 Brown B (2018). 'Dare to Lead: Brave Work. Tough Conversations. Whole Hearts', Penguin Random House UK.
2 Brown B (2012, p. 62). 'Daring Greatly: How the Courage to be Vulnerable Transforms the Way We Live, Love, Parent and Lead', Penguin Random House UK.
3 Brown B (2010). 'The Gifts of Imperfection: Let Go of Who You Think You're Supposed to Be and Embrace Who You Are', Penguin Random House UK.
4 Brown B (2018, p. 126). 'Dare to Lead: Brave Work. Tough Conversations. Whole Hearts', Penguin Random House UK.
5 Brown (2012). 'Daring Greatly: How the Courage to be Vulnerable Transforms the Way We Live, Love, Parent and Lead', Penguin Random House UK.
6 Hartling LM, Rosen W, Walker M & Jordan JV (2000). 'Shame and Humiliation: From Isolation to Relational Transformation', Wellesley Centers for Women, No. 88, https://www.humiliationstudies.org/documents/hartling/HartlingShameHumiliation.pdf Accessed 14.02.21.
7 Brown B (2012). 'Daring Greatly: How the Courage to be Vulnerable Transforms the Way We Live, Love, Parent and Lead', Penguin Random House UK.
8 Brown B (2018). 'Dare to Lead: Brave Work. Tough Conversations. Whole Hearts', Penguin Random House UK.
9 Lamia MC (2011). 'Shame: A Concealed, Contagious, and Dangerous Emotion', Psychology Today, https://www.psychologytoday.com/gb/blog/intense-emotions-and-strong-feelings/201104/shame-concealed-contagious-and-dangerous-emotion. Accessed 04.09.20.
10 Kammerer A (2019). 'Behaviour and Society: The Scientific Underpinnings and Impact of Shame', Scientific American, https://www.scientificamerican.com/article/the-scientific-underpinnings-and-impacts-of-shame/. Accessed 24.02.25.
11 Kammerer A (2019, no page reference). 'Behaviour and Society: The Scientific Underpinnings and Impact of Shame', Scientific American, https://www.scientificamerican.com/article/the-scientific-underpinnings-and-impacts-of-shame/. Accessed 24.02.25.
12 Kammerer A (2019). 'Behaviour and Society: The Scientific Underpinnings and Impact of Shame', Scientific American, https://www.scientificamerican.com/article/the-scientific-underpinnings-and-impacts-of-shame/. Accessed 24.02.25.
13 Brown B (2010). 'The Gifts of Imperfection: Let Go of Who You Think You're Supposed to Be and Embrace Who You Are', Penguin Random House UK.
14 Brown B (2010, p. 69). 'The Gifts of Imperfection: Let Go of Who You Think You're Supposed to Be and Embrace Who You Are', Penguin Random House UK.
15 Brown B (2010). 'The Gifts of Imperfection: Let Go of Who You Think You're Supposed to Be and Embrace Who You Are', Penguin Random House UK.

16 Brown B (2018). 'Dare to Lead: Brave Work. Tough Conversations. Whole Hearts', Penguin Random House UK.

17 Kammerer A (2019). 'Behaviour and Society: The Scientific Underpinnings and Impact of Shame', Scientific American, https://www.scientificamerican.com/article/the-scientific-underpinnings-and-impacts-of-shame/. Accessed 24.02.25.

18 Lond R, Nerys R & Loft P (2020). 'Bullying in UK Schools', House of Commons Briefing Paper 8812.

19 Education Support (undated). 'Bullying and Harassment', https://www.educationsupport.org.uk/resources/for-individuals/guides/bullying-and-harassment/#:~:text=In%20a%20survey%20carried%20out,from%20a%20range%20of%20sources. Accessed 04.08.22.

20 Hartling LM, Rosen W, Walker M & Jordan JV (2000). 'Shame and Humiliation: From Isolation to Relational Transformation', Wellesley Centers for Women, No. 88, https://www.humiliationstudies.org/documents/hartling/HartlingShameHumiliation.pdf Accessed 14.02.21.

21 Brown B (2017). 'Daring Classrooms', SXSWedu Keynote, https://www.youtube.com/watch?v=DVD8YRgA-ck. Accessed 30.01.22.

22 Brown B (2017). 'Braving the Wilderness: The Quest for True Belonging and the Courage to Stand Alone', Penguin Random House UK.

23 Brown B (2012, p. 74). 'Daring Greatly: How the Courage to be Vulnerable Transforms the Way We Live, Love, Parent and Lead', Penguin Random House UK.

24 Brown B (2012, p. 61). 'Daring Greatly: How the Courage to be Vulnerable Transforms the Way We Live, Love, Parent and Lead', Penguin Random House UK.

6 Safety Issues

Physical Safety

Keeping order in classrooms is a demonstration of professional reliability which is an important component of teacher trustworthiness. As a participant stated, 'I thought teachers were supposed to protect you and like sort things out, watch over you'.[1] If teachers are unable to manage classroom behaviour, students feel physically unsafe which diminishes their trust and increases feelings of anxiety. Emotional stress from perceived threats to safety can be overwhelming, particularly for students who live in chaotic or unsafe environments or those for whom traumatic memories are triggered by loss of adult control. Whilst behaviour management can be viewed through a range of different lenses, the technique presented in this section is a simple and effective tool which is arguably useful for all teachers once they have completed the preliminary greeting, seating, starter routines and addressed any obvious student issues.

Practitioners who are blessed with the presence to still a challenging class are arguably like the gods of the profession; gaining the attention of a class is undoubtedly a sought-after and desirable professional skill which, if not mastered, can trigger high levels of vulnerability. However, classroom presence can be learned using an acting technique commonly taught in drama schools. Several years ago, I was fortunate to come across Rob Salter's website (now inactive) pointing to *the correct use of status* as the single, most effective way to achieve *instant presence*, an invaluable skill for effective classroom management. The ability to proactively *raise or lower status* in the classroom and become a *status master* is the aim of the technique, and this is how it works in three simple steps:

Step 1: Be on stage. The front of the class is typically the stage, and the student seating area is the auditorium.

Step 2: Stand up straight, shoulders down and take a couple of deep breaths. This will help you feel calm and project your voice. Use a

DOI: 10.4324/9781003466963-7

simple consistent command such as 'silence' or a countdown. Project your voice, speak calmly and clearly *three ... two ... one.*

Step 3: STAY COMPLETELY STILL. This is *crucial* and communicates to the students that you are serious. Use your head and eyes to scan the room, resting on students who are not yet compliant. If they fail to respond, maintain a calm tone, say their name to gain eye contact, and use a command – 'silence'. REMAIN ABSOLUTELY STILL. You will feel as much as hear the moment when to begin to speak.

The importance of waiting until the class is silent cannot be under-estimated but equally begin teaching promptly once all students are attentive. If students start to talk, stop and repeat the technique. Initially it may take a few attempts but persevere as the benefits are significant. The goal is to develop the confidence to raise or lower status as required, to *keep order* in high-status mode, to *build relationships* in low-status mode. I have sometimes observed teachers remaining on stage during a whole lesson; however, supporting students in the auditorium is important, and it is possible to alternate between the two. For example, if there are students in the classroom off-task or disrupting others, stand up and use a high-status approach with them: 'on-task', 'remain seated', 'not appropriate'... 'thank you'. Teachers who play only low status give the message *I don't know how to raise my status, if I am nice to you, hopefully you will like me and not abuse me.* Teachers who play only high status give the message *I do not know how to lower my status, I do not care about or like you, I am here to scare you.* A high-status persona is essentially an effective method of *acting strict* rather than *reacting emotionally* to students who may be trying to gain mastery over teachers. In some classes, it may be necessary to identify students who are the leaders of the pack so to speak – because it is with them that it will be important to use the technique well, establish status mastery and build relationships.

It is crucial that keeping order is carried out using a calm, rather than confrontational, approach in order for students to feel sufficiently safe to learn. When students overstep a line or when difficult messages need to be given, they may temporarily transfer their dislike of the message onto the person delivering it. This may feel vulnerable, but it's perfectly acceptable for students to dislike teachers at times; keeping order using a status master approach will ultimately build student trust. Hard conversations (with students or staff) invariably trigger vulnerability, but it gets easier with practice. Being clear about class management boundaries in the right way (modelling calm and stillness), at the right time (choose your battles wisely), is a prerequisite for learning and trust. Some teachers have the gift of using humour to do so.

Status Tips:

- **Breaking eye contact** can be high status but do not be tempted to look back at the student, even for a moment.
- **'End of conversation'** followed by total stillness is a good alternative to the broken record technique.
- **'Don't even think about it'** (followed by total stillness) works well if you spot someone about to misbehave.
- **Presentation:** sloppy appearance communicates that I do not pay attention to details and will let things go.
- **Organisation:** poor planning communicates that I may be asking you to be disciplined but you cannot rely on me to lead by example.
- **Over-use of sanctions** communicates that I do not have the ability to change your behaviour and will use my power to sanction.

Evaluate your current status. If you consider your presentation is low status, *practise* the status master techniques, preferably with a colleague, then use them. (A quick, whole staff or department session on practising voice projection may be time well spent.) If you spend most of your time on stage and rely heavily on your natural ability to be high status, consider changing your practice. Start moving into the auditorium and connecting with students – they will welcome you.

> Sometimes I feel worried when I put my hand up with strict teachers – if I get it wrong they won't like me. I don't think they need to be strict; they need to have trust in the children. When they have trust in the children the children will trust them back.[2]

Salter's books[3,4] provide more detailed information about status mastery techniques and approaches.

Emotional and Psychological Safety

The terms *emotional* and *psychological* safety are often used interchangeably; however, the term psychological safety has gained prominence as a result of Edmondson's research into the relationship between teamwork and medical errors in hospitals.[5] Initially puzzled by data showing that the most effective medical teams made the most clinical mistakes, Edmondson experienced a eureka moment when she realised that the teams with the highest error counts did not in fact *make* more mistakes, they *reported* more mistakes because they worked together in a climate of psychological safety. When people believe they will be given the benefit of the doubt and are not hindered by interpersonal fear, all group members feel safe to speak up, question and share information freely, including those who lack confidence.[6]

Giving others the benefit of the doubt and adopting a mindset of extending the 'most generous interpretation possible to the intentions, words and actions of others'[7] fosters emotional and psychological safety, a component of trustworthiness that participants considered essential to trust development. Experience suggests that teachers can tend to assume the worst, as illustrated by academically able, emotionally literate participant reports about repeated incidents of *not being believed* leading to anger and distrust. Arguably, humans benefit far more from believing others despite occasionally getting duped[8]; moreover, schools rarely get it wrong when serious incidents occur and investigations are carried out. As a participant noted, the problem is that teachers can behave as if they are 'judge, jury and executioner'.[9]

The significance of psychological safety for schools is highly relevant to group situations such as classrooms where there are additional dynamics to consider. Although individuals' feelings inevitably vary, the classroom climate has the greatest impact on the psychological safety of a class or group. Crucial to psychological safety is the *teacher's public response* to students when they make mistakes, struggle to learn, speak out or exhibit unacceptable behaviours. Participants concurred that 'Teachers are not always careful about what other people would think'.[10] When dealing with challenging situations, remember the eyes and ears of the other students are on the teacher, and the messages that matter to them are these: *If I slip up, if I get it wrong how will I be treated by this teacher?* Alternatively: *This teacher is not bothering to find out what really happened, she is blaming others carelessly, I can't trust her.*

Giving students the benefit of the doubt, extending the most generous interpretation possible to their words and actions *until and unless there is evidence to the contrary*, fosters a climate of emotional and psychological safety. In practising this approach, I have found that students invariably take steps to disclose what was actually going on, usually choosing to do so in private. There is an apt expression which comes to mind pertinent to the risk of making assumptions: to *ASSUME* makes as *ASS* out of *YOU* and *ME*. Noticing a tendency to assume is arguably a self-reflective tool from which open-mindedness and wise judgement can arise.

Self-Protection

When emotional safety is at risk or when feeling vulnerable, people use a range of unhealthy self-defence mechanisms to protect themselves. *Masks*, *armour* and *shields* are metaphors Brown uses to describe common, self-defensive patterns of behaviour people use to avoid emotional discomfort. Often, young people are not yet practised or comfortable using emotional defences (although some students learn from an early age and the older they get, the more comfortable they become). For adults, however, self-defensive behaviours can become indistinguishable from their identity and invariably their use is a barrier to authenticity and trust.[11] Participants identified the following self-protective tendencies they had encountered their teachers using at school[12]:

- Careless and repeated use of sanctions.
- Shouting at students.
- Rudeness.
- Interrupting and not listening, thinking they know best.
- Laughing with other students when a student gets an answer wrong.
- Criticising students ideas.
- Public sarcasm causing other students to name call and make fun.
- Picking on students, including those who find things hard.
- Blaming/accusing students carelessly which makes students not bothered to learn.
- Avoidance – not taking action when needed.

The problem with using defence mechanisms is that they do not eliminate vulnerability and invariably lead to distrust. Avoiding, numbing or offloading vulnerability not only compromises the experience of positive emotions but also makes it more likely that the supressed emotions will resurface.[13] Discharging vulnerability is common and harmful in hierarchical environments where power differentials exist, and Brown substantiates 16 organisational 'armoured leadership' styles including 'leading for compliance and control', and using 'power over' arising from threats to ego or self-worth to avoid vulnerability or shame.[14] However, invulnerability does not protect people from shame, conversely it assures it.[15] Although 'the good news is the teacher makes the difference, … the bad news is the teacher makes the difference',[16] and in schools, adults are far less likely to be held accountable than students for behaviours which undermine emotional safety and trust. Shouting and careless use of sanctions were behaviours which particularly concerned participants:

> If a teacher shouts at a student and it's like constant, the student could have, like um thoughts in their brain saying, 'Oh this teacher doesn't like me, this teacher doesn't want me to be here'.[17]

Developing the courage to be vulnerable enables teachers and students alike to take off their masks, abandon their armour and put down their shields. New learnings create opportunities for approaches which generate kinder, more engaging and inclusive methods to educate students and experience points to the reciprocal impact on staff being equally beneficial. In organisations, 'tackling a difficult problem is often a matter of seeing where the high leverage lies' and making changes that lead to lasting, significant improvement.[18] Ultimately, operationalising trust is a *high leverage* strategy which requires deep organisational learning, but it is also a smart skill which stands the test of time. Moreover, experience overwhelmingly points to existing good practice in teacher-student trust development in many schools which is a supporting factor in implementing trust initiatives.[19]

Try These: (Appendix E: Emotional Safety and Self-Protection)

- Be alert to the self-protection mechanisms students may be using to avoid feeling vulnerable, especially when learning. Remain curious, empathise and offer support.
- Model emotional regulation and be consistent in your responses. If you feel angry, walk away and breathe. Shouting and careless use of sanctions will undermine trust. If you are drawn into an argument, try telling students you are *choosing to let them have the last word*. Remember the eyes and ears of all students are on you.
- If students are angry give them time and space. Talk exacerbates emotional arousal and challenge, especially for students who struggle with language. If students are acting out give directed time out as discreetly as possible, preferably accompanied, even by a responsible peer. On average, it takes an angry student half an hour before their rational brain starts functioning.
- Avoidance is a common response to feeling afraid or worried and is an armoured behaviour. Always take the presentation of fear or anxiety seriously; never downplay it or assume students are making up excuses simply to avoid doing something.
- Always address students behaviours which fall outside organisational values, either witnessed or reported by students. Sometimes, it may seem easier to avoid acting, but student safety is a priority and every member of the community shares the responsibility to uphold values. State the boundaries clearly and calmly using a status master approach.
- Remember to greet students at the classroom door which promotes students' emotional safety and readiness for learning.
- Never dismiss an idea or say it's wrong. Instead ask *Why do you think that?* or *Nearly there*.[20]
- Be *relatable* and make time to get to know your students. Students will be more confident to get things wrong when they believe you will try and help them to get things right *just like a family would*.[21]

Notes

1 Byrnell VH (2019, Appendix M, p. 3). 'Academic Paper and Conference Presentation', St Mary's University.
2 Byrnell VH (2019, Appendix M, p. 3). 'Academic Paper and Conference Presentation', St Mary's University.
3 Salter R (2016). 'The Behaviour Blueprint: What Works in the Classroom and Why', self-published.
4 Salter R (2016). 'Classroom Presence Pocketbook', Teachers' Pocketbooks.
5 Edmondson AC (2019). 'The Fearless Organisation: Creating Psychological Safety in the Workplace for Learning, Innovation, and Growth', John Wiley & Sons, Inc.
6 Edmondson AC (2019). 'The Fearless Organisation: Creating Psychological Safety in the Workplace for Learning, Innovation, and Growth', John Wiley & Sons, Inc.
7 Brown B (2017, p. 39). 'Braving the Wilderness: The Quest for True Belonging and the Courage to Stand Alone', Penguin Random House UK.
8 Levine TR (2020). 'Duped: Truth-Default Theory and the Social Science of Lying and Deception', The University of Alabama Press.
9 Byrnell VH (2019). 'Academic Paper and Conference Presentation', St Mary's University.
10 Byrnell VH (2019, Appendix M, p. 3). 'Academic Paper and Conference Presentation', St Mary's University.
11 Brown B (2018). 'Dare to Lead: Brave Work. Tough Conversations. Whole Hearts', Penguin Random House UK.
12 Byrnell VH (2019). 'Academic Paper and Conference Presentation', St Mary's University.
13 Brown B (2018). 'Dare to Lead: Brave Work. Tough Conversations. Whole Hearts' Penguin Random House UK.
14 Brown B (2018, p. 76). 'Dare to Lead: Brave Work. Tough Conversations. Whole Hearts' Penguin Random House UK.
15 Brown B (2018, p. 119). 'Dare to Lead: Brave Work. Tough Conversations. Whole Hearts' Penguin Random House UK.
16 Jones J (2009, p. 96). 'The Magic-Weaving Business: Finding the Heart of Learning and Teaching', Leannta Publishing.
17 Byrnell VH (2019, Appendix M, p. 4). 'Academic Paper and Conference Presentation', St Mary's University.
18 Senge PM (2006, p. 64). 'The Fifth Discipline: The Art and Practice of the Learning Organisation', Random House Business Books.
19 Trowler PR, Saunders M & Knight PT (2002). 'Change Thinking, Change Practices: A Guide to Change for Heads of Department, Subject Centres and Others Who Work "Middle-Out"', LTSN Generic Centre.
20 Byrnell VH (2019, Appendix M, p. 3). 'Academic Paper and Conference Presentation', St Mary's University.
21 Byrnell VH (2019, Appendix M, p. 3). 'Academic Paper and Conference Presentation', St Mary's University.

7   Imagine the Possibilities

In the 1960s, Piaget developed the idea that in order for children to understand something, they must construct it for themselves, reinvent it or symbolise it which requires *the capacity for imagination*.[1] Aligned with contemporary understandings of vulnerability Piaget also identified that *in defence mode*, the capacity for imagination is compromised and students struggle to make connections, symbolise, think creatively and learn.[2] However, the development of students' imaginative capacity is not only compromised by invulnerability arising from emotional defences. As Sir Ken Robinson argued, 'the countries that have done well on the standards agenda are often paying a heavy price in a loss of creativity, motivation, and engagement in students, the very qualities on which personal, cultural, and economic vitality now depend'.[3] The leaning towards uniformity within the English educational environment through the goal of standardisation is arguably outdated and needs revision. Business leaders around the world have identified the need to re-think educational priorities; for example, the World Economic Forum identifies a range of key capabilities that are increasingly highly sought and all developed by various forms of imaginative play in and out of school including *problem solving, sociability, creativity, curiosity, communication, adaptability* and *leadership*.[4]

In 2015, Pasi Sahlberg and William Doyle switched their respective home countries, Finland and the US, and began a five-year international research journey into the power of play to transform the learning experiences of children at school.[5] Play in education means 'those engaging activities, both self-guided and guided by adults that allow a child to use her or his creativity, curiosity and imagination in a process that can have powerful intellectual and physical benefits for the child'.[6] In research studies, experiments and real-life school experiences around the world, different forms of play integrated into both primary and secondary settings are associated with benefits relating to cognitive, social, emotional and physical development. For example, in north Texas and Oklahoma, four 15-minute unstructured breaks every day resulted in

DOI: 10.4324/9781003466963-8

strong improvements in academic performance and behaviour for thousands of low- and middle-income students; in Singapore, academic ranking and over-testing inducing stress in primary school students is shifting towards a new model of childhood exploration, experimentation and discovery.[7] Evidence increasingly points to the importance of developing students creativity and imagination as demonstrated by the internationally recognised success achieved by Finland based on an educational model where students in all key stages are required to have at least one hour of unstructured play a day.

Significantly, improvements in student functioning through educational play have been demonstrated in many key areas including *attention, memory, perspective-taking, cooperating, problem-solving, creativity, self-regulation, empathy, resilience and feelings of well-being.*[8] Regardless of the occupations students may choose, these are attributes which will benefit them and are highly desirable educational outcomes that equip them to succeed. Although teachers do not have the influence needed to bring about changes to the structure of the school day, they *can* change the climate in their classrooms. Developments in neuroscience show that fun, laughter and playfulness release oxytocin, a hormone which helps to counter the impact of the stress hormone cortisol.[9] Moreover, studies consistently demonstrate that superior learning and motivation arise from playful, as opposed to instructional, approaches to learning.[10]

Self-Orientated Learning Environments (SOLE) are a creative learning approach to consider incorporating into teaching routines. Award-winning educationalist Sugata Mitra placed a computer in the wall of an Indian slum situated next to his office and observed that children could teach each other almost anything.[11] The results were astonishing, dispelling the seeming imbalance of intellectual capability between economically advantaged and disadvantaged children in India. The learning capacity of children was further increased by the presence of a supportive adult who required no teaching or subject expertise; their job was simply to inject connection and positivity, using words such as *amazing, fantastic, wow!* The SOLE learning community is free to join, demonstrates how to run SOLE sessions and provides subject-related questions that will keep even the most disaffected students engaged, as experienced when teaching maths to disadvantaged KS4 students. Professor Sugata Mitra was named in the 2022 Brock Prize in Education Innovation Laureate for his transformational work in rethinking the way children learn.

Curriculum and classroom practices have not changed significantly in decades, and Jones argues that 'the track record of schools is not encouraging'; that for schools to become 'key players in the regeneration of our communities, our country and society as a whole', they need to become 'hotbeds of creativity, centres of imagination and champions of change'.[12] Although it is encouraging to find contemporary research which points to the importance of learning through play to promote engagement, inclusion and skills development,[13] there is as yet insufficient agreement or action to implement effective play pedagogies beyond preschool age. There is arguably a pressing need to reenvisage and reform traditional educational models which are not yet adapting to develop skills and attributes that will benefit all young people and economies in the future.

Try These (Appendix F: Imagine the Possibilities)

- Aim to have fun with students in lessons. This starts by greeting students with a smile and adopting a positive, encouraging attitude towards all students.
- Try introducing lessons with play-based approaches to learning at key times of the day when students can struggle to remain focused. There are play-based approaches which facilitate skill-building in every subject – for example, strategy, literacy, maths and science games as well as creative challenges. Experience suggests there is a great deal to be learned about students from their play and they engage and work harder when you need them to, as a consequence.
- Log onto the SOLE website https://startsole.org/, and if possible timetable some information and communication technology-based lessons where your students can engage in self-orientated learning, focusing on big questions relevant to your subject.
- Consider showing students funny video clips for light relief or teach students a subject-related song. It is heartwarming to hear classes of secondary students singing enthusiastically in their language lessons and invariably their teachers are also smiling. Singing does not need to be limited to language lessons; students enjoy maths rap too.
- Refrain from depriving systemically vulnerable students of break times unless there is a recognised risk to safety; typically, the students most in need of the benefits of play are those who miss out the most, both in home and school environments.

Notes

1 Piaget J & Inhelder B (1969). 'The Psychology of the Child', Basic Books.
2 Piaget J & Inhelder B (1969). 'The Psychology of the Child', Basic Books.
3 Robinson K (2014). 'Can Creativity Be Taught', The Brainwaves Video Anthology, https://www.youtube.com/watch?v=vIBpDggX3iE. Accessed 24.02.25.
4 World Economic Forum (2018). 'The Top 10 Job Skills of Tomorrow – And How Long it Takes to Learn Them', https://www.weforum.org/agenda/2020/10/

top-10-work-skills-of-tomorrow-how-long-it-takes-to-learn-them/. Accesssed 24.02.25.

5 Sahlberg P & Doyle W (2019). 'Let the Children Play: How More Play Will Save Our Schools and Help Children Thrive', Oxford University Press.

6 Sahlberg P & Doyle W (2019, p. 50). 'Let the Children Play: How More Play Will Save Our Schools and Help Children Thrive', Oxford University Press.

7 Sahlberg P & Doyle W (2019). 'Let the Children Play: How More Play Will Save Our Schools and Help Children Thrive', Oxford University Press.

8 Sahlberg P & Doyle W (2019). 'Let the Children Play: How More Play Will Save Our Schools and Help Children Thrive', Oxford University Press.

9 Whitaker D (2021). 'The Kindness Principle: Making Relational Behaviour Management Work in Schools', Independent Thinking Press.

10 Whitebread, D, Neale D, Jensen H, Liu C, Solis SL, Hopkins E, Hirsh-Pasek K & Zosh JM (2017). 'The Role of Play in Children's Development: A Review of the Evidence (Research Summary)', The Lego Foundation, https://cms.learn ingthroughplay.com/media/esriqz2x/role-of-play-in-childrens-development-review_web.pdf. Accessed 16.05.24.

11 Mitra S (2013). 'Build a School in the Cloud', TED2013, https://www.ted.com/talks/sugata_mitra_build_a_school_in_the_cloud?language=en. Accessed 24.02.25.

12 Jones J (2009, p. 45). 'The Magic-Weaving Business: Finding the Heart of Learning and Teaching', Leannta Publishing.

13 Parker R, Thomsen BS & Berry A (2022). 'Learning Through Play at School – A Framework for Policy and Practice', Frontiers in Education, Vol. 7, p. 751801, https://doi.org/10.3389/feduc.2022.751801.

8 Non-Judgement Is Wise Judgement

Teachers typically make numerous judgements on a daily basis which contributes to the inherent vulnerability of the profession because decision-making induces uncertainty and the risk of getting it wrong.[1] *Non-judgement* does not mean refraining from making value judgements and decisions based on what practitioners value in organisational life, rather it means refraining from making *moralistic* judgements about students as individuals, notwithstanding their *behaviours* may be unethical. The distinction is an important one because 'moralistic judgements imply wrongness or badness on the part of people who don't act in harmony with our values'[2] and as identified, when students receive messages which lead them to believe they are inherently *flawed*, it increases the risk of disconnection and shame. Labelling, criticism and comparisons are all likely to be received as moralistic judgement leading to reciprocal distrust:

> When someone tells you that you're something, you feel that you are that or did it. The teacher thinks of you in a different way than you think of yourself and you start to feel like they don't trust you.[3]

When addressing student behaviours which do not align with organisational values, non-judgement (also a key empathy attribute) begins with *practising curiosity* because curiosity expands the gap between observation and reaction, helps people to see situations more clearly and promotes perspective-taking and connection.

> If you are curious then you are automatically being non-judgemental. If you can be non-judgemental then you will allow a child to remain engaged with you and they are therefore less likely to escalate their response and become more distressed.[4]

Curiosity feels vulnerable because 'it requires us to surrender to uncertainty', and as a result, people tend to choose *certainty* and *knowing*

DOI: 10.4324/9781003466963-9

over curiosity and learning.[5] As yet, there are no definitive answers about how to develop curiosity, but there are a growing number of researchers who believe that 'curiosity and knowledge-building grow together'.[6]

The challenge for practitioners is to pay attention to the judgement language they use, particularly with students who they struggle to build relationships with. Some students are able to evoke intensely negative feelings in their teachers, and a valuable technique I learned from an educational psychologist, which is commonly practised by therapists, is the technique of *transference*. Aligned with empathetic connection, the ability to *assess how an individual is making us feel in the moment* is undoubtedly a skill that teachers can also learn. Transference requires the discipline to practice self-awareness and recognise the feeling being triggered by a student's behaviour. This feeling is actually the way the student is feeling, only more acutely and often without the capacity to communicate or self-regulate that feeling. Shifting the focus from the behaviour itself to *reading* the behaviour by seeking to understand the underlying feeling is curiosity practice. Understanding that rudeness or non-compliance in students is generally a response to underlying feelings of anger or deep-seated fear facilitates relational behaviour management and responses aligned with *educationally wise judgement* 'which lies at the very heart of what goes on in the classroom and in the relationships between teachers and students'.[7]

Furthermore, promoting *responsibility* for behavioural misconduct *requires* a non-judgemental approach because the act of recognition and responsibility gives rise to an acknowledgement of weakness, failure, getting it wrong.[8] Shame-prone students will struggle to take responsibility, and they will defend themselves against vulnerability and shame unless they receive empathy, non-judgement and support:

Mr Smith actually makes you see the bad side of *what you did* (italics added). Yeh, Mr Smith helps you understand.[9]

Inclusive practice challenges teachers to exercise educationally wise judgement with students they find difficult to work with but remember, their presentations may be a cover for vulnerability and shame. Students are adept at sensing teachers' dislike, and shields and armour can become a familiar mantle unless we remain curious, seek to connect and understand:

It's easy to judge. It's more difficult to understand. Understanding requires compassion, patience and a willingness to believe that good hearts sometimes choose poor methods. Through judgement we separate. Through understanding we grow.[10]

Try These (Appendix G: Non-Judgement Is Wise Judgement)

- Practice empathy, curiosity and educationally wise judgement 'I notice you're struggling to do as asked, tell me more, tell me how this is for you'?
- Notice the judgement habits you practise with students and monitor your language carefully. Behaviours may fall outside organisational values, but students need to feel valued regardless. Remember that *good hearts sometimes choose poor methods.*
- When student behaviours are ethically questionable, begin conversations along the lines 'I know you have a good heart and this behaviour (be explicit) is not aligned with your values, can you tell me what's going on?'
- Consider displaying the following poem in your classroom and staffroom to promote the trustworthy characteristic of non-judgement. If shame is present, there is always a risk of unhealthy moralistic judgement by adults and students alike.

Judge Softly

Pray, don't find fault with the child who limps
Or stumbles along the road,
Unless you have worn the shoes she wears
Or struggled beneath her load.

There may be tacks in her shoes that hurt
Though hidden away from view,
Or the burden she bears, placed on your back
Might cause you to stumble too.

Don't smear the child who's down today
Unless you have felt the blow
That caused her fall, or felt the shame
That only the fallen know.

You may be strong, but still the blows
That were hers, if dealt to you
In the self-same way, at the self-same time
Might cause you to stagger too.

Don't be too harsh with the child who sins
Or pelt her with words or stones
Unless you are sure – yes, double sure
That you have no sins of your own.

For you know, perhaps, if the tempter's voice
Should whisper as soft to you
As it did to her when she went astray,
'Twould cause you to falter, too.

Try walking a mile in the child's shoes,
Don't criticise, blame or accuse,
And find a way to take the time
To reflect on your own views.

I believe you'd be surprised to see
You've been narrow-minded, even blind.
For there're children from all walks of life
With too much worry on their minds.

We'll be known forever by the tracks we leave
In other people's lives.
So open your heart, put on her shoes
And see through the child's eyes.

(Source: Version of original poem by
Lathrap M T (1895) 'Judge Softly')

Notes

1 Kelchtermans G (2009). 'Who I Am in How I Teach Is the Message: Self-Understanding, Vulnerability and Reflection', *Teachers and Teaching: Theory and Practice*, Vol. 15, No. 2, pp. 257–272.
2 Rosenberg MB (2003). 'Non Violent Communication: A Language of Life', 2nd Edition, PuddleDancer Press.
3 Byrnell VH (2019, Appendix M, p. 7). 'Academic Paper and Conference Presentation', St Mary's University.
4 Whittaker D (2021, p. 69–70). 'The Kindness Principle: Making Relational Behaviour Management Work in Schools', Independent Thinking Press.
5 Brown B (2015, p. 52). 'Rising Strong: If We Are Brave Enough, Often Enough, We Will Fall', Penguin Random House UK.
6 Brown B (2015, p. 55). 'Rising Strong: If We Are Brave Enough, Often Enough, We Will Fall', Penguin Random House UK.
7 Biesta GJJ (2013, p. 130). 'The Beautiful Risk of Education', Routledge.
8 Whittaker D (2012). 'The Kindness Principle: Making Relational Behaviour Management Work in Schools', Independent Thinking Press.
9 Byrnell VH (2019, Appendix M, p. 7). 'Academic Paper and Conference Presentation', St Mary's University.
10 Zantamata D (2020) 'Happiness in Your Life', https://www.thehiyl.com/2020/10/its-easy-to-judge.html. Accessed 27.03.25.

9   Gratitude Gateways

An identified decline in children's mental health points to the intense pressures facing students in today's world along with the need to cultivate resilience. Not only are students subject to increasing academic pressures but technological advances and social media are the norm. Students are exposed to countless consumables, images and messages that increase their sense of *scarcity*, *envy* and *insecurity* as well as having access to information that necessitates keen powers of discernment. Living in a generation that tends to expect more alongside a climate of inequitable access to resources, it is easy to see how gratitude – feeling thankful and appreciating life's simple pleasures – is at risk of diminishing. A few years ago, a child and adolescent psychotherapist shared that a student referred to her was suffering from debilitating levels of anxiety resulting from the fear of achieving less than an A* in just one of her GCSE subjects and thereby disappointing her parents.

Cultivating gratitude practice in students is more important than practitioners might think as an aspect of inclusion because studies in psychology show that gratitude, especially expressing it to others, is linked to reductions in depressive symptoms, enhanced well-being, increased energy, life satisfaction, empathy, connection and joyfulness.[1] Joy is a deceptively vulnerable emotion because it is often accompanied by a sense of foreboding – an inner voice that prohibits continued joyfulness with thoughts or anxieties about impending doom.[2] Many people experience joyful moments in life, or reflect that everything is going well, only to be quickly followed by the thought that they need to prepare for the worst. The remedy to the vulnerability of foreboding joy is gratitude; it is recognising there is a risk of losing something precious and allowing yourself to notice the 'shiver of vulnerability …, to just sit with it and be grateful that you have something you want, in your hand, that it feels good to hold and recognise'.[3] Moreover, when people allow themselves the experience of joy, it helps to build a reservoir of resilience to draw from when times are difficult in the same way that practicing self-compassion builds a reservoir of empathy to extend to others.

DOI: 10.4324/9781003466963-10

Understanding the benefits of gratitude is typically an insufficient motivator for action however, and research points to a range of reasons why gratitude practice comes more easily to some people than others. Genetics and in particular the genes involved in the secretion of oxytocin and recycling of dopamine are significantly associated with the 'quality and frequency of expressions of gratitude' towards others.[4] Lower levels of oxytocin and dopamine have been found to result in a 'negativity bias' and a 'habit of neglecting positive aspects of life events and complaining about misfortunes'.[5] Fortunately, genetic differences in brain structure and activity which impact people's propensity for gratitude are not immutable, and intentional gratitude practice can result in long-term, advantageous physical changes to the brain. Likewise, a predisposition for emotions such as envy, self-interest or materialism can be counteracted by developing a habit of practising gratitude.[6]

The impacts of diminishing gratitude are not only on individual wellbeing but are more far reaching. The Education Reform Act 1988 gives priority to promoting amongst other aims, the *spiritual* and *moral* development of students. Whilst there is a larger debate about spiritual and moral development, it is notable that links between gratitude and spiritual and moral dimensions exist in history and are also a renewed topic of interest in academic writing today.[7] In Roman times, Cicero orated that 'gratitude is not only the greatest of virtues, but the parent of all others'.[8] Similarly, in the Doctrine of Virtue, the German philosopher Kant includes gratitude as 'one of the three primary ethical duties of love toward others'.[9] Arguably, the link between gratitude and the spirit is that both are expressed by internal and outward movements towards an object and pertain to 'the distinctive capacity of human beings to transcend the material and acquire a growing consciousness of themselves, not only as individuals, but also in relation to others and the world'.[10] The concept of spirituality emerged from Brown's research as a 'critical component of resilience and over-coming struggle'[11] pointing to links between resilience and gratitude as spiritual practice. Resilience necessitates foundational beliefs about the interconnectedness of human beings, and arguably gratitude practice towards others embraces a sense of this interconnectedness. There is perhaps a danger of contemporary technological societies setting their sights too low, focusing on the satisfaction of material needs without sufficient regard for the spiritual nature and needs of human beings.[12]

Experience points to gratitude as a transformative virtue over time; it cultivates a demeanour of positivity and appreciation – for connection, learning, beauty, human transcendence, the list is individual and endless. Gratitude practice enables people to *count their blessings* amidst the everyday travails of life and to appreciate aspects of people they may otherwise take for granted; if mastered, gratitude can even nurture the power to transform life's obstacles into opportunities, arguably a highly advantageous attribute for educators.

Try These (Appendix H: Gratitude Gateways)

- Create an ethos of gratitude in your school by remembering to thank colleagues and staff repeatedly, from management to caretakers and cleaning staff. In emails and all communications, try to communicate at least one positive message.
- Find as many reasons as you can to thank students for what they do and say. Thank them for their time, contributions, good behaviours, politeness, patience, turning up, being on time, etcetera.
- Introduce gratitude practice with students. For example, in tutor time or in personal, social and health education lessons, introduce a daily/ weekly gratitude session – a sharing event, or a note/letter writing exercise to express appreciation for someone or something in their lives.
- Expose students to the situations of other young people in the world who live in life-limiting or dangerous circumstances, not with the intention of making comparisons, but because studies suggest that contemplating endings makes people more grateful for the life they currently have. There is a caveat, as always, for the need for sensitivity towards students who have personal experiences of grief or loss.
- Model the ability to savour positive experiences with students – thank them for their contribution to making lessons memorable or enjoyable.
- Demonstrate impeccable manners and speak to students as you would speak to a respected colleague or friend to reinforce respect and appreciation for others.
- Develop the habit of thinking of something to be grateful for each day. For example, if you wake up feeling tired or out of sorts, 'think of what a precious privilege it is to be alive, to breathe, to think, to enjoy, to love'.[13]

Notes

1 Froh JJ, Sefick WJ & Emmons RA (2008). 'Counting Blessings in Early Adolescents: An Experimental Study of Gratitude and Subjective Well-Being', *Journal of School Psychology*, Vol. 46, No. 2, pp. 213–233.
2 Brown B (2018). 'Dare to Lead: Brave Work. Tough Conversations. Whole Hearts', Penguin Random House UK.
3 Brown B (2018, p. 83). 'Dare to Lead: Brave Work. Tough Conversations. Whole Hearts', Penguin Random House UK.
4 Allen S (2018, npr). 'Greater Good Science Centre: Magazine: Science-Based Insights for a Meaningful Life', https://greatergood.berkeley.edu/ article/item/why_is_gratitude_so_hard_for_some_people#:~:text=Our%20

genes%20and%20our%20brains,as%20%E2%80%9Cthieves%20of%20
thankfulness.%E2%80%9D. Accessed 25.02.25.

5 Allen S (2018, npr). 'Greater Good Science Centre: Magazine: Science-Based Insights for a Meaningful Life', https://greatergood.berkeley.edu/article/item/why_is_gratitude_so_hard_for_some_people#. Accessed 25.02.25.

6 Allen S (2018). 'Greater Good Science Centre: Magazine: Science-Based Insights for a Meaningful Life', https://greatergood.berkeley.edu/article/item/why_is_gratitude_so_hard_for_some_people#. Accessed 25.02.25.

7 Wirtz D, Fordon CL & Stalls J (2014). 'Gratitude and Spirituality: A Review of Theory and Research', Religion and Spirituality Across Cultures, Vol., 9, pp. 287–301, Springer.

8 Timmons M (2017, p. 241). 'The Moral Significance of Gratitude in Kant's Ethics', Significance and System: Essays on Kant's Ethics, Oxford Academic, https://doi.org/10.1093/acprof:oso/9780190203368.003.0002.

9 Timmons M (2017, p. 241). 'The Moral Significance of Gratitude in Kant's Ethics', Significance and System: Essays on Kant's Ethics, pp. 13–49, Oxford Academic, https://doi.org/10.1093/acprof:oso/9780190203368.003.0002.

10 Byrnell VH (1994, p. 5). 'Spiritual and Moral Development: Education for Life or an Anathema?', Institute of Education.

11 Brown B (2015, p. 10). 'Rising Strong: If We Are Brave Enough, Often Enough, We Will Fall', Penguin Random House UK.

12 Byrnell VH (1994). 'Spiritual and Moral Development: Education for Life or an Anathema?', Institute of Education.

13 Aurelius M (161–180 AD). 'Meditations', Penguin Classics.

10 Support Matters

The willingness to ask for help and support was one of the top answers that leadership groups gave when asked what team members do to earn their trust.[1] Participants concurred that 'If you're able to ask for help from someone then that means you trust them'.[2] Equally, it follows that school leaders asking for help or support promotes their team members' trust in them; however, for leaders, asking for help can feel acutely vulnerable given that leadership denotes recognised levels of expertise and competence. Consequently, in hierarchical organisations, there is a need to guard against cultural defensiveness – having to know the answers and solutions rather than being curious and open to learning:

> School trains us never to admit that we do not know the answer, and most corporations reinforce that lesson by rewarding the people who excel in advocating their views, not inquiring into complex issues … Even if we feel uncertain or ignorant, we learn to protect ourselves from the pain of appearing uncertain or ignorant.[3]

Experience suggests there are many students and adults too, who are unable to ask for help or support when they need it most.

Given that asking for help or support is high on the agenda of trustworthy behaviours to operationalise trust, the question arises of how this translates into reciprocal trust-building when it is teachers who are typically in the position of providing help and students who need the help? Of course, teachers can and do find ways to ask students for help, and it is beneficial to find as many opportunities as possible to do so; however, the tables are often turned when it comes to asking for help from students, especially from those who are most in need of connection and trust. For systemically vulnerable students, asking for help can feel especially vulnerable, triggering shame messages connected to unworthiness or hidden flaws. Arguably to mitigate the teacher–student positional disparity, participants repeatedly pointed to *unconditional*

DOI: 10.4324/9781003466963-11

teacher support as a key trust-building characteristic in schools[4]; they trusted teachers who were consistently willing to:

- Support students who struggle more.
- Help students no matter how many times help is needed.
- Give up time, pay attention to details.
- Provide sheets that help students who work slower.
- Stay behind to help individual students.
- Walk around and explain in more detail.
- Give feedback that questions, explains, helps you understand.
- Always try to help students learn.
- Use revision methods that help you learn like a normal lesson so you don't even feel you're revising.
- Respond to emails from students which saves time and enables them to remember the help given.

Support really helps, sometimes for a long time.[5]

Research on inclusive schooling in a municipality of Sweden, which transformed its position from bottom to top of the national school league tables, points to promoting help and support as a key inclusion initiative.[6] Driven by the headteacher, the school fostered a culture of helpfulness where students were strongly and consistently encouraged to ask for help and help each other. Students were prompted to think in terms of *receiving help and support as a right* which they should persist in, until satisfied. Consequently, it seemed that all students 'developed a kind of interdependence – with students and with staff – that felt safe to them and which allowed them to seek and receive support'.[7] The reference to safety is pertinent, not only in respect of mitigating the vulnerability required to ask for help, but also because if people judge themselves for needing help, subconsciously they are just as likely to judge those who need help.[8] When follow-up research was conducted with participants who had transitioned to upper secondary schools, the confidence to seek help and support had persisted over time, with students continuing to benefit.

Teacher support needs to be unconditional – patient, non-judgemental and empathetic; passed through a kind word or deed, a choice to connect, listen and learn, trust in action. Support given in these ways is vulnerable because teachers are often pressurised and time-limited, but still they are called to give more because the child in front of them needs them to care that much. As a participant noted about a teacher who all participants concurred garnered high levels of trust, 'Mr Joseph just doesn't give up on the child. Mr Joseph still tries more and more to help the child'.[9] Inevitably, there are students whose needs prove too complex for them to flourish in mainstream schools without specialist provision available, but it remains important to 'never get tired of doing the little things for others because sometimes those little things occupy the biggest parts of their hearts'.[10] Through unconditional support, practitioners can be confident that they have given their best to help the child in front of them.

Try These (Appendix I: Support Matters)

- Discuss as a class how students find it easiest to ask for help and display the ideas they come up with. Systemically vulnerable students are likely to continue to find asking for help challenging, so check in with them as often as you can and be ready to offer support.
- Share with students the things you find difficult and need help with. Ask students for their help and support whenever an opportunity arises.

> When I've needed help she'll help me or if she needs help, I'll help her.[11]

- Use students' natural inclination to be helpful as a strategy; helping can boost their self-esteem by giving them a sense of purpose and value.

Supporting SEND Students

In the existing climate of resource scarcity, increasing numbers of students with special educational needs and disabilities (SEND) in mainstream education inevitably leads to calls for more staff and resources. The challenges of building trust and supporting students is undoubtedly significant in classes where up to a quarter of students can be identified with SEND. However, it is noteworthy that small group interventions have significantly more impact than an extra person in the classroom, so deploying learning support staff needs careful consideration to ensure SEND students do not miss out on teaching specialism.[12] There are a number of inconspicuous reasons why supporting SEND students presents increased challenges for teachers. For example, heightened levels of learning and social anxiety trigger increased teacher vulnerability because anxiety, like shame, is a contagious emotion. Furthermore, teacher anxiety can be exacerbated by a lack of self-efficacy which requires, at the very least, adequate training, understanding and information as discussed further in Chapter 13.

Students with social, emotional and mental health (SEMH) concerns, particularly those with attention-deficit hyperactivity disorder (ADHD) warrant particular consideration, as they are at increased risk of escalating sanctions and school exclusion.[13] Around 25% of the adult prison population are identified with ADHD, many of whom also have undiagnosed learning needs.[14] The percentage is likely to be even higher, given the number of students who remain undiagnosed in school settings. Arguably, both medical and teacher training has neglected a systematic study of ADHD[15] which, like autism, is neurodevelopmental in nature and can be comorbid with it. On a daily basis, teachers and support staff struggle to meet the needs of neurodiverse students in homogenic school systems that are generally neither adaptive nor well suited to promote their access to learning. Increased understanding of neurodiversity is needed to help teachers empathise and make adaptations because invariably neurodiverse students are profoundly grateful and enabled to learn when practitioners understand the challenges they face and support them positively.[16]

Research points to attention or inattention difficulties consistent with ADHD characteristics being symptomatic of *low dopamine levels* pointing to ADHD as a *dysfunction* rather than a deficit of attention.[17] This distinction is important because a specific difficulty students experience is when asked to *shift* attention, to *transition* between tasks and activities which is when support is most needed. As evidenced by Communicourt, a defendant 'had considerable difficulty switching his focus when asked to read written evidence on the stand, then struggled to hold information from that document in his mind when answering questions arising from it'.[18] Equally, ADHD students may unconsciously create disruption as a way to *stimulate* their dopamine levels, and when their behaviours are triggered by neurological factors they themselves are unable to regulate or understand, they experience a deep sense of shame.[19] Most of the time, ADHD students are focused almost entirely on what is wrong with them and are constantly fearful of being exposed in some way or other.[20] The emotional pain, heightened anxiety and shame underlying ADHD are often missed in the self-defensive behaviours students typically present with. Thus, reinforcing boundaries requires an empathetic, rather than a punitive approach because overt disapproval and shaming in the classroom are common for behaviours ADHD students do not consciously choose.[21]

Furthermore, ADHD students may *seem* to be able to concentrate and attend perfectly well in one lesson, but present with distracting or impulsive behaviours in another, leading teachers to believe they are choosing to behave this way. However, many people are unaware that ADHD students have an extraordinary energy and ability to hyperfocus in their field of interest, whereas what they find 'imobilisingly difficult is to arouse the brain's motivational apparatus in the absence of personal interest'.[22] Lack of concentration in subjects ADHD students struggle with may also be attributable in part to mental fatigue from the increased effort it takes to manage their symptoms. Depression is highly correlated with ADHD, and heightened anxiety can lead to more prominent and pronounced self-conscious symptoms such as ticks and impulsivity;

moreover, persistent restlessness often results in chronic sleeping difficulties and fatigue. Michael Phelps, for example, diagnosed with ADHD and one of the most highly decorated Olympians, was told by a teacher at school that *he would never amount to anything or achieve success*; after leaving school, he required treatment for depression.[23] As Dr Mate adduces from the school histories many adults with ADHD have reported to him, practitioners are sometimes unaware of 'their immense power to wound' or 'how deep classroom-inflicted emotional hurts can go'.[24] Teachers who can maintain trusting, nonjudgemental relationships with ADHD students will invariably be rewarded with less disruption and longer attention spans because except in the most severe cases, their anxiety will reduce, and confidence increase. Ultimately, inclusion is not a destination but a journey of new learnings and possibilities to create inclusive schools where more students have a place to belong; after all, 'it is easier to build strong children than to repair broken men'.[25]

Tips for Working with Neurologically Diverse Students (Appendix I: Support Matters)

- Building positive relationships is key to working successfully with students with ADHD; find out their interests and the people who are important to them, communicate genuine warmth and take opportunities to praise seemingly routine behaviours such as settling, shifting attention or ignoring distractions.
- When a relationship is built, be explicit in the way you connect with students. For example, 'I need you shift your attention now, I know this is what you find difficult, what support do you need to focus on the next task?' Or 'I notice you seem very tired today; I understand how that feels, try and relax and do the best you can'.
- ADHD and its associated anxiety can often be passed on genetically. Make specific efforts to build positive relationships with parents and carers and communicate positive feedback. This can help to reduce school-related anxieties in the home environment which are invariably passed on to students.
- Seat purposefully *in collaboration with* the student. Contrary to what teachers often insist on, some ADHD students are far more comfortable sitting at the back of classrooms where their anxiety levels are reduced.
- Be mindful that seemingly innocent peers know only too well how to distract and raise anxiety levels in ADHD students.
- Aim to stand close to ADHD students when speaking, whether at the front or back of the classroom. When necessary, attract the student's attention by using their name calmly and making eye contact. Be aware that students with comorbid autism may be unable to reciprocate eye contact.

- Allow fiddle objects, doodling or drawing, but remain calm and patient when directing students to start work – remember *shifting attention is their struggle* and this is when support is most needed.
- Give one instruction at a time and chunk tasks into achievable steps. Provide scaffolding and support to begin writing tasks (dysgraphia and processing difficulties affect 50% of ADHD students). The chunking strategy is recommended for all students affected by language or working memory difficulties and compromises none.
- Intervene early, at the first signs of impulsive, restless or distracting behaviours. You could try:

  - Giving a classroom responsibility.
  - Asking the student to run an errand for you – sometimes a prepared envelope to take to reception can work well if reception staff are briefed and willing.
  - ADHD students also frequently lose water bottles and get overheated, so allow them to get a drink of water.

- If school arrangements allow and symptoms are severe (sometimes, symptoms can vary according to the time of day), offer the option of working in a support room, presented as a positive choice. Students with ADHD often benefit from working in support rooms with access to lesson power points on laptops, as evidenced during the COVID pandemic. Be willing to listen to their suggestions about alternative ways to access learning successfully and permit rest breaks if practicable.
- If students become argumentative or aggressive, do not get drawn in – remember shame is a hallmark of ADHD. Use a strategy that works to give students time out to calm down whilst preserving their dignity. If possible, agree on a strategy collaboratively with the student in private.
- Sanctions may be necessary, but be realistic about their efficacy in changing behaviours. Building relationships will *always* be more successful and taking the time to meet with ADHD students 1:1 to discuss the best way to support them can produce unexpectedly positive results.
- See ADHD students as individuals with values and character traits that define them more than their neurological traits do. Few ADHD students will leave school without a battering to their self-esteem, and some degree of social rejection.[26]

Notes

1 Brown B (2017). 'Braving The Wilderness: The Quest for True Belonging and the Courage to Stand Alone', Penguin Random House UK.
2 Byrnell VH (2019, Appendix M, p. 2). 'Academic Paper and Conference Presentation', St Mary's University.
3 Senge PM (2006, p. 25). 'The Fifth Discipline: The Art and Practice of the Learning Organisation', Random House Business Books.

4 Byrnell VH (2019). 'Academic Paper and Conference Presentation', St Mary's University.
5 Byrnell VH (2019, Appendix M, p. 2). 'Academic Paper and Conference Presentation', St Mary's University.
6 Allan J & Persson E (2016). 'Students Perspectives on Raising Achievement through Inclusion in Essunga, Sweden', *Educational Review*, Vol. 68, no. 1, pp. 82–95, https://doi.org/10.1080/00131911.2015.1058752.
7 Allan J & Persson E (2016, p. 92). 'Students Perspectives on Raising Achievement through Inclusion in Essunga, Sweden', *Educational Review*, Vol. 68, no. 1, pp. 82–95, https://doi.org/10.1080/00131911.2015.1058752.
8 Brown B (2017). 'Braving The Wilderness: The Quest for True Belonging and the Courage to Stand Alone', Penguin Random House UK.
9 Byrnell VH (2019, Appendix M, p. 2). 'Academic Paper and Conference Presentation', St Mary's University.
10 Unattributed quote, https://www.passiton.com/inspirational-quotes/6016-never-get-tired-of-doing-little-things-for. Accessed 27.03.25.
11 Byrnell VH (2019, Appendix M, p. 2). 'Academic Paper and Conference Presentation', St Mary's University.
12 Education Endowment Foundation (2021). 'Teaching Assistant Interventions', https://educationendowmentfoundation.org.uk/education-evidence/teaching-learning-toolkit/teaching-assistant-interventions. Accessed 25.02.25.
13 DFE (2023). 'Suspension and Permanent Exclusion from Maintained Schools, Academies and Pupil Referral Units in England, Including Pupil Movement'.
14 Communicourt (2022a). 'ADHD & Criminal Justice: Understanding the Iceberg', https://www.communicourt.co.uk/news/adhd-criminal-justice-under standing-the-iceberg/#:~:text=The%20prevalence%20of%20Attention%20 Deficit,Young%20%26%20Cocallis%2C%202021. Accessed 25.02.25
15 Mate G (1999a). 'Scattered: How Attention Deficit Disorder Originates and What You Can Do about It', Penguin Group.
16 Mahony E (2019). 'Better Late Than Never: Understand, Survive and Thrive Midlife ADHD Diagnosis', Trigger.
17 Mahony E (2019). 'Better Late Than Never: Understand, Survive and Thrive Midlife ADHD Diagnosis', Trigger.
18 Communicourt (2022, no page reference) 'ADHD & Criminal Justics: Understanding the Iceberg', https://www.communicourt.co.uk/news/adhd-criminal-justice-understanding-the-iceberg/#:~:text=The%20prevalence%20of%20 Attention%20Deficit,Young%20%26%20Cocallis%2C%202021). Accessed 27.03.25.
19 Mahony E (2019). 'Better Late Than Never: Understand, Survive and Thrive Midlife ADHD Diagnosis', Trigger.
20 Mahony E (2019). 'Better Late Than Never: Understand, Survive and Thrive Midlife ADHD Diagnosis', Trigger.
21 Mate G (1999). 'Scattered: How Attention Deficit Disorder Originates and What You Can Do about It', Penguin Group.
22 Mate G (1999, p. 14). 'Scattered: How Attention Deficit Disorder Originates and What You Can Do about It', Penguin Group.
23 Mahony E (2019). 'Better Late Than Never: Understand, Survive and Thrive Midlife ADHD Diagnosis', Trigger.
24 Mate G (1999, p. 214). 'Scattered: How Attention Deficit Disorder Originates and What You Can Do about It', Penguin Group.
25 Mapp S, Gabel SG (2019, citing Douglass F, 1855) 'It is Easier to Build Strong Children than to Repair Broken Men', J.Hum.Rights Soc.Work 4, 145-146, https://link.springer.com/article/10.1007/s41134-019-00106-z#citeas, Accessed 27.03.25.
26 Mahony E (2019). 'Better Late Than Never: Understand, Survive and Thrive Midlife ADHD Diagnosis', Trigger.

Part II

11 Gritty Governance

Political governance arguably plays a critical role in shaping educational and cultural change in the state maintained system. Typically, there are practitioners in all schools who build trust and make a genuine difference to student outcomes, yet their reach has limited impact on the overall effectiveness of a school or on broader educational concerns. Teachers operate within a context, and it is ultimately system-led, whole school influences that are key to maximising equitable educational outcomes for all students.[1,2] Solutions that address only the symptoms of a problem rather than the fundamental cause tend to have short-term benefits at best[3] as signified by ongoing teacher recruitment and retention difficulties despite incentives on the government agenda for a number of years.[4] Whilst the intricacies of public sector policy-making need to be recognised, there is arguably a pressing need to understand more about systemic barriers which contribute to low staff morale, inequity and exclusionary school practice to create the conditions for sustainable improvement in England's schools.

Institutional Trust

Governance of public sector organisations is a complex undertaking for many reasons, not least because conflicting objectives often arise between stakeholder powers and the 'ill-defined subject of the public interest'.[5] For example, when allocating resources, there is inherent tension between the need for economy and efficiency whilst also satisfying the purpose which a public sector organisation seeks to achieve – its effectiveness. This tension is exacerbated by corresponding values of equity and equality to ensure that public worth is available to all citizens including marginalised groups.[6] Overarching public sector objectives are by nature value driven, and values are not only subject to incompatibility issues, but they can also be incommensurable, meaning that when a conflict occurs, there is no overriding value to resolve the issue; thus,

DOI: 10.4324/9781003466963-13

governance decisions invariably involve contending with diverse and often conflicting values.[7]

Complex ethical decision-making triggers high levels of vulnerability due to uncertainty, the risks of being wrong and the emotional tension which conflicting ethical values can provoke.[8] It is questionable to what extent the implications of this aspect of governance are addressed given the particular challenges vulnerability presents in governance where 'decision-makers are strongly averse to being vulnerable'.[9] As discussed in Part I, unhealthy defence mechanisms in response to vulnerability or shame can result in dysfunction, distrust and alienation; equally, government policy directives can be a source of vulnerability and defence mechanisms for stakeholders.[10] Governance is after all a human endeavour pointing to the need for a sound grasp of matters pertaining to relational trust and its barriers to guard against power misuse (see Chapter 12). The known benefits of relational trust for organisational and economic advantage are gaining momentum, making it expedient for those in positions of power to understand and model trust-building skills and competencies.[11,12]

As guardians of the public funds, setting direction and steering the course, ministers assume significant responsibility in exercising their powers.[13] As indicated, other stakeholders are impacted directly or indirectly by collective government decisions and the reciprocal nature of trust creates an interdependent relationship between governments and public servants.[14] There is naturally a greater degree of separation between government ministers and public servants than between public servants within organisations, so typically trust is not practised in an interpersonal way. Thus, in governance, the concept of *institutional trust* is relevant whereby trust develops or breaks down according to 'relational signalling' based on interpretations of underlying intentions and implications.[15] Values, resourcing, communication, policy implementation and effectiveness all contribute to relational signalling of both affective and evaluative components of trust.[16] As noted in Part I, trustworthy characteristics may vary according to context-specific variables or terminology, and public sector trust in governance is a developing area of research.[17] A synopsis of identified components for evaluating relational signals of institutional trust between governance and public sector organisations is shown in Table 11.1 although it is not intended to be a definitive list.[18,19,20]

Internationally, trust in governments by stakeholders is found to be lower than stakeholder trust in other key public sector institutions, and declining levels of trust are particularly pronounced in Western Europe and the US.[21] In the context of education, it is relevant that the primary stakeholders are children aged 3–18 and thus outcomes relating to education are not fully realised or assessable within the natural

Table 11.1 Components of Institutional Trust

Trustworthy Components	Relational Signalling
Integrity	Upholding ethical values, principles and norms, especially relating to fairness, honesty and self-interest.
Resourcing	Sufficiency and appropriateness of resources to deliver the purposes set by the state.
Reliability	Ability to assess the needs of the service and anticipate evolving challenges.
Openness	Sharing information accurately, consulting, listening to stakeholders, ensuring equal opportunities for participation of diverse groups.
Effectiveness	Stakeholder satisfaction and quality of outcomes.

term of a government. As a result, resourcing and policy initiatives can be subject to short-termism leading to cycles of uncertainty and vulnerability for other affected stakeholders.[22] Simultaneously long-term strategic direction can be difficult to sustain through changes of governmental ideology, so there is an increased risk of piecemeal policy rather than systems thinking in pursuit of reliability and effectiveness.[23] Furthermore, differing *stakeholder* ideology and regional and school differences inevitably lead to divergence of opinion, pointing to the context-sensitive nature of stakeholder trust in governance. These complex interrelations and variables suggest a greater risk of fragmentation and distrust across the system which impacts the equitable delivery of services to systemically vulnerable stakeholders more than those possessing agency to source alternative providers. Trust breakdown is more prevalent among socio-economically disadvantaged groups; thus, equity must be a key consideration for governments.[24]

Educational Governance in England

Political governance has remained a dominant influence in the history of education in the UK since 1721.[25] The current system of state-maintained education in England comprises an inefficient dual system with 50% of all schools in academy trusts and local authorities supporting a diminishing number of schools with declining resources.[26] The fragmentation of the system can be traced back to the Education Reform Act 1988 which signalled a change in educational direction, reducing the powers of local authorities and enhancing the powers of central government.[27] Known as the *new public management model*, this centralist educational paradigm was rooted in international trends towards globalisation in pursuit of efficiency and growth.[28,29,30] Consequently, governments were required to make strategic choices between 'cost resource savings' versus improving performance through 'resource investment'.[31] In England, new public management in education signalled an era of standardisation and accountability in a drive to improve efficiency and make cost resource savings. A national curriculum, school league tables, performance-related pay and Ofsted (Office for Standards in Education, Children's Services and Skills) were introduced, driving increased competition between schools and implementing punitive consequences for those failing to meet expected standards. Arguably education became akin to a commodity where the efficiency of service delivery determined its effectiveness,[32] although differing levels of resourcing reflected differing strategic choices according to the political ideologies of governments in office. By 2011, adverse working conditions accentuated by inequity in disadvantaged areas led to teacher dissatisfaction and evolving recruitment and retention concerns.

In 2013, a key issue identified in the Organisation for Economic Co-operation and Development's (OECD) Survey of Adult Skills was that on average young adults in England were no more literate or numerate than their grandparents' generation.[33] The Education Minister pointed to a 'long tail of low attainment' and accelerated a process of delegating 'supported autonomy' to school leaders whilst simultaneously introducing even more rigorous standards and accountability measures at a time of continuing public sector austerity, largely neutralising the accompanying fair National Funding Formula.[34] The government retained substantial control over school standards while further advancing the academisation of state schools, thereby removing them from local authority management and shifting towards a school-led, self-improving system.[35] The autonomy afforded to academy trusts has enabled some to benefit from economies of scale and innovate where it matters most.[36] For example, Dixons Academy Trust has successfully challenged educational and social disadvantage in Northern England, through a strong mission to maximise attainment, value diversity, develop character and build cultural capital.[37] However, evidence suggests that scaling good practice across the system has always been difficult to achieve and that managing expansion successfully is an identified concern for the Chief Executive Officer of Dixons.[38]

To date, evidence suggests that high-performing multi-academy trusts (MATs) are a minority because more often than not, lack of system coherence leaves students and practitioners vulnerable to the negative impacts of market ideology. Although it can be argued that accountability in the English system has led to a significant fall in the number of very low-performing schools, over the long term, the initially attractive benefits of standardisation and efficiency can drive the best professionals out, stifle innovation and lead to stagnation.[39] Moreover, the majority of students with systemic vulnerabilities in the special educational needs and disabilities (SEND) category remain the responsibility of local authorities whose powers are limited as they have no say about place numbers or admissions in academies and no powers to co-ordinate services.[40] Whilst recent OECD data suggests that literacy and numeracy scores in the UK have improved, the share of young adults whose highest level of education has a vocational orientation remains significantly below both the European Union and OECD averages.[41] A skills deficit in the system points to a need to rethink approaches to curriculum and assessment which are currently intended to compete with the world's best education systems rather than to value multiple intelligences and promote student engagement.[42] Thus, the existing approach to curriculum and assessment arguably lacks a coherent career development model that enables young people to 'understand their skills, the broader labour market and the range of career pathways' available to them.[43]

Stress Indicators

In the current educational climate, teachers are leaving the profession at the highest rate in four years linked to a range of identified issues including[44]:

- Workload.
- Government initiatives and policy changes.
- Pressures relating to pupil outcomes or inspection.
- Pay restraint.
- Erosion of external services.

Maintaining the confidence of the workforce is crucial to a sustainable system,[45] and teachers are rarely misguided; they enter the profession well aware that teaching is demanding work, and pay scales are incommensurate with similar levels of responsibility in other sectors. Critical recruitment and retention issues signal breakdowns across key components of institutional trust – for example, signalling pertaining to levelling up[46] is significantly at odds with the impact of system reforms or the efficacy of proposals to address it, undermining institutional integrity. Inadequate levels of support for increasing numbers of systemically vulnerable students are widespread with local authorities lacking the resources or powers to meet their needs effectively.[47] Increasingly experience points to cuts to external services resulting in teachers assuming responsibility for additional roles such as SEND specialist, social worker, therapist and family support for which they are not trained. Moreover, a system perceived as failing to meet need arguably contributes negatively to professionals' feelings of value. Compounding problems further a weak regulatory set-up for academies with powers and responsibilities fundamentally misaligned creates inefficiency and provides inadequate mechanisms to intervene in underperforming multi academy trusts:

> For each of the responsibilities set out in the 2016 white paper there is a misalignment that can lead to a less equitable system, and which means worse outcomes for some of the most vulnerable young people in the education system.[48]

Regardless of the pandemic acting as a catalyst, the relational signalling pertaining to the reliability of governments' ability to accurately assess the needs of the service and anticipate stressors has been an underlying concern for practitioners for years.[49,50] Post-pandemic signals of distrust are now evident across increasing numbers of stakeholders, and most concerning is the impact on the students themselves. An investigation by the Centre for Social Justice found that[51]:

- Persistent absence rates have been increasing since 2019, and post-pandemic, they have risen to record levels of 26.4%.
- Absence rates are higher in secondary schools (31.5%) with 30% of students living in the most disadvantaged areas versus 14.3% in the most affluent areas.
- The most commonly cited reasons for absence are:
  - Anxiety-related mental health concerns alongside inadequate mental health provision.
  - Undiagnosed and unmet SEND needs.
  - Disengagement with the curriculum.
- Nearly one in two young people aged 15–16 do not see secondary school as an enjoyable or meaningful experience.

Sufficient funding is a precondition for providing high-quality education with early years intervention considered to be a key determinant of equity in education.[52] However, data points to an illogical national funding formula where resource per disadvantaged pupil falls as deprivation rates rise.[53] For example, in real terms, the Early Years Pupil Premium was 2% lower in 2023–2024 than in 2017–2018, whilst core funding for all disadvantaged pupils including those with SEND is set to fall by 22% with the most deprived secondary schools experiencing the greatest cuts.[54] It is therefore unsurprising that belated financial intervention is insufficient to remedy high financial anxiety levels across the whole education sector in England with tensions now focused on ways to save money in the face of prolonged government underinvestment.[55] Simultaneously, governmental drive on ever higher academic targets[56] adds weight to the argument that revising standards may be a more sustainable option which would not necessarily lead to 'students becoming less educated, teachers less professional or leaders less motivated;' rather, it suggests that 'the standards being raised may be the wrong standards' to achieve the learning and change that will engender the greatest benefits to society.[57]

The Way Forward

Recently, government white papers have emphasised the importance of research-based evidence to inform policy.[58] Although this is a welcome shift, the scope for criticality of review in the light of ideological attachments and sensitivities is unclear. Generally, literature on good governance already subscribes to the idea that focusing on efficiency and results increases the risk of neglecting other dimensions such as effectiveness.[59] As professionals and many parents understand, educating and caring for students is 'too complex a process to be measured by quantitative metrics alone'.[60] Whilst comparisons between countries need to be contextually understood, arguably evidence from those who have resisted the global educational reform movement and implemented alternative ideas is a helpful starting point from which to evaluate the bigger picture and the direction of travel needed. A well-documented example is Finland which bucks the trend both in marketisation of education and stakeholder perceptions of trust in governance.[61,62] Table 11.2 summarises key contrasts in the evolution of the Finnish and English education systems.

Table 11.2 Comparison of English and Finnish Educational Goals

Educational Goals	
England	Finland
Increased competition	Increased collaboration
Standardised curriculums with a focus on core subjects	Personalised, creative and holistic curriculums
Test-based accountability	Trust-based responsibility valuing teacher professionalism and autonomy
Opportunity for all (with insufficient resourcing)	Quality and equity (with fair, targeted resourcing)

In a post-war era in England, the Education Act 1944 was considered to be a seminal piece of legislation commanding rarely achieved, cross-party political support; it aimed to provide for all students:

> Equal opportunity for physical, intellectual, social and spiritual development which while taking advantage of the practical interests of the pupils should make *the full development of personality the first objective* [italics added].[63]

Although the inequitable tripartite system in place at the time proved too challenging to reform, prioritising the development of character in young people is arguably as important today as it was 80 years ago, pointing to a deeper meaning of learning which awakens shared intuition about what it means to be human and contribute to the generative process of lifelong learning.[64] In a post-pandemic climate, widespread economic pressures are affecting the majority of OECD countries resulting in additional tensions on educational systems. The record of governance in England points to an existing system already experiencing elevated levels of inequity and distrust, and therefore the way forward is likely to be particularly challenging. In the complex, ambiguous and volatile arena of education, dictates arising from fluctuating political ideology inevitably reduce stability, consistency and clarity of purpose. For example, after just one year in office, the previous government passed the Education Act 2011 which simultaneously abolished[65]:

- The General Teaching Council for England
- The School Support Staff Negotiating Body
- The Qualifications and Curriculum Development Agency
- The Young People's Learning Agency

A decade on the result is a confusing and inequitable system relying on a disproven belief that it is possible to successfully scale up best practice across the entire system without the regulatory powers to achieve this. In view of the quality of outcomes that it is possible to achieve, evidenced by a number of existing school organisations, reform which delegates regulatory powers to a National Education Service would be a visionary and courageous undertaking but also potentially transformative. Establishing a regionally diverse group of experienced and skilled educational leaders, working collaboratively with government and external providers to synthesise lessons from the past and oversee and steer direction for the future, seems a sensible move towards long-term system coherence, equity and quality.

'Systems thinking' is a discipline for seeing wholes rather than parts which helps to ameliorate the sense of powerlessness which can sometimes be triggered when confronted with high levels of complexity, thus reducing confidence and responsibility.[66] The success of systems thinking lies in identifying where the high leverage lies and in change which seeks to understand underlying patterns behind events and details.[67] Underlying patterns in education emerge through synthesis of a range of factors across all parts of the system including the *nature* of quality in outcomes sought. An over emphasis on academic targets risks limiting the potential and expectations for young people because 'most of what pupils need to learn in school cannot be formulated as a clear standard'.[68] Arguably an emerging pattern is the importance of relational and institutional trust to quality outcomes across a range of educational fields, and contemporary research points to an actionable way forward.[69] A focus on trust development not only addresses matters relating to values and learning, but also makes economic sense because the resource costs of trust breakdown are far reaching and high, placing additional stressors on other key services in the societal ecosystem. Sufficient funding, although necessary, is not the sole solution because existing problems will inevitably resurface in the long term unless high leverage strategies are identified and implemented.[70]

Sometimes the keys are indeed under the streetlamp; but very often they are off in the darkness. After all, if the solution *were* easy to see or obvious to everyone, it probably would already have been found.[71]

Notes

1 Fullan M (2009). 'The Principal and Change', The Challenge of Change: Start School Improvement Now, pp. 55–77, Corwin Press.
2 Mincu M (2022). 'Why Is School Leadership Key to Transforming Education? Structural and Cultural Assumptions for Quality Education in Diverse Contexts', *Prospects*, Vol. 52, p. 231, https://www.ncbi.nlm.nih.gov/pmc/articles/PMC9628287/pdf/11125_2022_Article_9625.pdf.
3 Senge P.M (2006, p. 103). 'The Fifth Discipline: The Art and Practice of the Learning Organisation', Random House Business Books.
4 Bottery M (2004). 'Trust: Its Importance for Educators', *Management in Education*, Vol. 18, No. 5, pp. 6–10, https://doi.org/10.1177/0892020605018000502.
5 Lynch R (2015). 'Government, Public Sector and Not-for-Profit Strategies', Strategic Management, Seventh Edition, pp. 597–611, Pearson Education.
6 Lynch R (2015). 'Government, Public Sector and Not-for-Profit Strategies', Strategic Management, Seventh Edition, pp. 597–611, Pearson Education.
7 De Graff G & Paanakker H (2014). 'Good Governance: Performance Values and Procedural Values in Conflict', *American Review of Public Administration*, Vol. 45, pp. 1–18, https://www.researchgate.net/publication/274519594_Good_Governance_Performance_Values_and_Procedural_Values_in_Conflict. Accessed 26.04.24.
8 Brown B (2018). 'Dare to Lead: Brave Work. Tough Conversations. Whole Hearts', Penguin Random House UK.

9 Diong KS, Foong SY & Sambasivan M (2018, p. 51). 'Relational Signalling in Governance Mechanisms and Trust Building', *Asian Journal of Accounting and Governance*, Vol. 9, pp. 49–61, https://journalarticle.ukm.my/19707/1/19378-90566-1-PB.pdf. Accessed 08.05.24.

10 Homes K, Clememt J & Albright J (2013). 'The Complex Task of Leading Educational Change in Schools', *School Leadership & Management*, Vol. 33, No. 3, pp. 270–283, https://doi.org/10.1080/13632434.2013.800477.

11 Cerna L (2014). 'Trust: What It Is and Why It Matters for Governance and Education', OECD Education Working Papers No. 108, https://doi.org/10.1787/5jxswcg0t6wl-en.

12 Frei X & Morriss A (2020). 'Begin with Trust: The First Step to Becoming a Genuinely Empowering Leader', Harvard Business Review, https://hbr.org/2020/05/begin-with-trust. Accessed 11.05.24.

13 Lynch R (2015). 'Government, Public Sector and Not-for-Profit Strategies', Strategic Management, Seventh Edition, pp. 597–611, Pearson Education.

14 Bottery M (2003). 'The Management and Mismanagement of Trust', *Educational Management and Administration*, Vol. 31, No. 3, pp. 245–261.

15 Cerna L (2014, p. 20). 'Trust: What It Is and Why It Matters for Governance and Education', OECD Education Working Papers No. 108, https://doi.org/10.1787/5jxswcg0t6wl-en.

16 OECD (2021). 'Building Trust to Reinforce Democracy: Main Findings from the 2021 OECD Survey on Drivers of Trust in Public Institutions', https://www.oecd-ilibrary.org/sites/b407f99c-en/1/3/1/index.html?itemId=/content/publication/b407f99c-en&_csp_=c12e05718c887e57d9519eb8c987718b&itemIGO=oecd&itemContentType=book. Accessed 05.05.24.

17 Diong KS, Foong SY & Sambasivan M (2018, p. 51). 'Relational Signalling in Governance Mechanisms and Trust Building', *Asian Journal of Accounting and Governance*, Vol. 9, pp. 49–61, https://journalarticle.ukm.my/19707/1/19378-90566-1-PB.pdf. Accessed 08.05.24.

18 Schoorman FD, Mayer RC & Davis JH (2007). 'An Integrative Model of Organisational Trust; Past, Present, and Future', *Academy of Management Review*, Vol. 32, No. 2, pp. 344–354, https://www.jstor.org/stable/258792?seq=1.

19 Kavanagh J, Carman KG, DeYoreo M, Chandler N & Davis LE (2020). 'The Drivers of Institutional Trust and Distrust: Exploring Components of Trustworthiness', RAND Corporation, https://www.rand.org/pubs/research_reports/RRA112-7.html. Accessed 08.05.24.

20 OECD (2021). 'Building Trust to Reinforce Democracy: Main Findings from the 2021 OECD Survey on Drivers of Trust in Public Institutions', Accessed 05.05.24.

21 Cerna L (2014). 'Trust: What It Is and Why It Matters for Governance and Education', OECD Education Working Papers No. 108, https://doi.org/10.1787/5jxswcg0t6wl-en.

22 Lynch R (2015). 'Government, Public Sector and Not-for-Profit Strategies', Strategic Management, Seventh Edition, pp. 597–611, Pearson Education.

23 Lynch R (2015). 'Government, Public Sector and Not-for-Profit Strategies', Strategic Management, Seventh Edition, pp. 597–611, Pearson Education.

24 OECD (2021). 'Building Trust to Reinforce Democracy: Main Findings from the 2021 OECD Survey on Drivers of Trust in Public Institutions', Accessed 05.05.24.

25 Gillard D (2018). 'Education in the UK: The History of Our Schools, Colleges and Universities', https://www.education-uk.org/history/timeline.html. Accessed 28.01.24.

26 Freedman S (2022). 'The Gove Reforms a Decade On: What Worked, What Didn't, What Next?', The Institute for Government, https://www.institutefor government.org.uk/publication/gove-school-reforms. Accessed 15.05.24.

27 Woods PA, Simkins T, Donnelly C, Hamilton T, Jones K, Potter I, Torrance D (2020). 'Educational Leadership, Management and Administration in the United Kingdom: A Comparative Review', BELMAS Project Report, https:// www.belmas.org.uk/publications/. Accessed 17.09.21.

28 Bottery M (2004). 'The Impact of Standardisation and Control', The Challenges of Educational Leadership, Sage, pp. 77–98.

29 Fisher T (2008). 'The Era of Centralisation: The 1988 Education Reform Act and its Consequences', Vol. 50, No. 2, FORUM.

30 Sahlberg P (2021). 'Finnish Lessons 3.0: What Can the World Learn from Educational Change in Finland', Teachers College Press.

31 Lynch (2015, p. 592) 'Government, Public Sector and Not-for-Profit Strategies', Strategic Management, Seventh Edition, pp. 597–611, Pearson Education.

32 Sahlberg P (2021). 'Finnish Lessons 3.0: What Can the World Learn from Educational Change in Finland', Teachers College Press.

33 OECD (2013). 'Skills Outlook 2013: First Results from the Survey of Adult Skills, https://read.oecd-ilibrary.org/education/oecd-skills-outlook-2013_ 9789264204256-en#page1. Accessed 15.05.24.

34 DFE (2016, p. 8 & 16). 'DFE Strategy 2015–2020: World-class Education and Care', https://assets.publishing.service.gov.uk/media/5a801b00e5274a2 e8ab4e373/DfE-strategy-narrative.pdf. Accessed 28.01.24.

35 Freedman S (2022). 'The Gove Reforms a Decade On: What Worked, What Didn't, What Next?', The Institute for Government, https://www.institutefor government.org.uk/publication/gove-school-reforms. Accessed 15.05.24.

36 Woods PA, Simkins T, Donnelly C, Hamilton T, Jones K, Potter I, Torrance D (2020). 'Educational Leadership, Management and Administration in the United Kingdom: A Comparative Review', BELMAS Project Report, https:// www.belmas.org.uk/publications/. Accessed 17.09.21.

37 Dickens J (2022). 'Luke Sparkes, Chief Executive, Dixons Academies Trust', Schools Week, https://schoolsweek.co.uk/our-students-leave-with-the-power ful-knowledge-they-can-challenge-the-elite/. Accessed 10.05.24.

38 Freedman S (2022). 'The Gove Reforms a Decade On: What Worked, What Didn't, What Next?', The Institute for Government, https://www.institutefor government.org.uk/publication/gove-school-reforms. Accessed 15.05.24.

39 Dickens J (2022). 'Luke Sparkes, Chief Executive, Dixons Academies Trust', Schools Week, https://schoolsweek.co.uk/our-students-leave-with-the-power ful-knowledge-they-can-challenge-the-elite/. Accessed 10.05.24.

40 Freedman S (2022). 'The Gove Reforms a Decade On: What Worked, What Didn't, What Next?', The Institute for Government, https://www.institutefor government.org.uk/publication/gove-school-reforms. Accessed 15.05.24.

41 OECD (2023). 'Education at a Glance 2023 OECD Indicators', https://www. oecd-ilibrary.org/docserver/e13bef63-en.pdf?expires=1708349355&id=id&a ccname=guest&checksum=6ED6782FA104B42100D6A58BBDC60284. Accessed 15.05.24.

42 Zemanik M (2022). 'What Is the Scale and Impact of Graduate Overqualification in Scotland?', Chartered Institute of Personnel and Development, https://community.cipd.co.uk/cipd-blogs/b/scotland_the_blog/posts/what-is-the-scale-and-impact-of-graduate-overqualification-in-scotland#. Accessed 15.04.24.

43 Zemanik M (2022, npr). 'What Is the Scale and Impact of Graduate Over-qualification in Scotland?', Chartered Institute of Personnel and Development, https://community.cipd.co.uk/cipd-blogs/b/scotland_the_blog/posts/what-is-the-scale-and-impact-of-graduate-overqualification-in-scotland#. Accessed 15.04.24.

44 Martin M (2023). 'How England Lost its Teachers – And How it Can Get Them Back', Times Educational Supplement Analysis, https://www.tes.com/magazine/analysis/general/teacher-recruitment-retention-crisis-solution. Access date: 01.02.24.

45 Bottery M (2012). 'Leadership, the Logic of Sufficiency and the Sustainability of Education', *Educational Management, Administration & Leadership*, Vol. 40, No. 4, pp. 449–463, https://doi.org/10.1177/1741143212438220.

46 H M Government (2022). 'Opportunity for All: Strong Schools with Great Teachers for Your Child', https://www.gov.uk/government/publications/opportunity-for-all-strong-schools-with-great-teachers-for-your-child. Accessed 25.02.25.

47 Freedman S (2022). 'The Gove Reforms a Decade On: What Worked, What Didn't, What Next?', The Institute for Government, https://www.institutefor government.org.uk/publication/gove-school-reforms. Accessed 15.05.24.

48 Freedman S (2022, p. 20). 'The Gove Reforms a Decade On: What Worked, What Didn't, What Next?', The Institute for Government, https://www.instituteforgovernment.org.uk/publication/gove-school-reforms. Accessed 15.05.24.

49 Bottery M (2004). 'The Impact of Standardisation and Control', The Challenges of Educational Leadership, Sage, pp. 77–98.

50 Bottery M (2012). 'Leadership, the Logic of Sufficiency and the Sustainability of Education', *Educational Management, Administration & Leadership*, Vol. 40, No. 4, pp. 449–463, https://doi.org/10.1177/1741143212438220.

51 The Centre for Social Justice (2023). 'Lost and Not Found: How Severe Absence Became Endemic in England's Schools', https://www.centreforsocialjustice.org.uk/library/lost-and-not-found. Accessed 25.02.25.

52 OECD (2023). 'Education at a Glance 2023 OECD Indicators', https://www.oecd-ilibrary.org/docserver/e13bef63-en.pdf?expires=1708349355&id=id&accname=guest&checksum=6ED6782FA104B42100D6A58BBDC60284. Accessed 15.05.24.

53 Drayton E, Farquharson C, Ogden K, Sibieta L, Tahir I & Waltmann B (2023). 'Annual Report on Education Spending in England: 2023', Institute for Fiscal Studies, https://ifs.org.uk/publications/annual-report-education-spending-england-2023#. Accessed 18.05.24.

54 Drayton E, Farquharson C, Ogden K, Sibieta L, Tahir I & Waltmann B (2023). 'Annual Report on Education Spending in England: 2023', Institute for Fiscal Studies, https://ifs.org.uk/publications/annual-report-education-spending-england-2023#. Accessed 18.05.24.

55 Dickens J (2022). 'Luke Sparkes, Chief Executive, Dixons Academies Trust', Schools Week, https://schoolsweek.co.uk/our-students-leave-with-the-powerful-knowledge-they-can-challenge-the-elite/. Accessed 10.05.24.

56 Ofsted Guidance (2023, p. 220 & 223). https://www.gov.uk/government/publications/school-inspection-handbook-eif/school-inspection-handbook-for-september-2023. Accessed 25.05.24.

57 Bottery M (2012). 'Leadership, the Logic of Sufficiency and the Sustainability of Education', *Educational Management, Administration & Leadership*, Vol. 40, No. 4, pp. 449–463, https://doi.org/10.1177/1741143212438220.

58 H M Government (2022). 'Opportunity for all: strong schools with great teachers for your child', E02727891 978-1-5286-3239-3, https://assets.

publishing.service.gov.uk/media/62416cb5d3bf7f32add7819f/Opportu
nity_for_all_strong_schools_with_great_teachers_for_your_child__print_ver
sion_.pdf. Accessed 26.04.24.

59 De Graff G & Paanakker H (2014). 'Good Governance: Performance Values and Procedural Values in Conflict', *American Review of Public Administration*, Vol. 45, pp. 1–18, https://www.researchgate.net/publication/
274519594_Good_Governance_Performance_Values_and_Procedural_
Values_in_Conflict. Accessed 26.04.24.

60 Sahlberg P (2021). 'Finnish Lessons 3.0: What Can the World Learn from
Educational Change in Finland', Teachers College Press.

61 Sahlberg P (2021). 'Finnish Lessons 3.0: What Can the World Learn from
Educational Change in Finland', Teachers College Press.

62 OECD (2021). 'Building Trust to Reinforce Democracy: Main Findings from
the 2021 OECD Survey on Drivers of Trust in Public Institutions', Accessed
05.05.24.

63 London County Council (1947, p. 25). 'Replanning London Schools', The
London County Council.

64 Senge PM (2006). 'The Fifth Discipline: The Art and Practice of The Learning
Organisation', Random House Business Books.

65 UK Public General Acts (2011). 'Education Act 2011', https://www.legislation.
gov.uk/ukpga/2011/21#. Accessed 25.02.25.

66 Senge PM (2006, p. 68). 'The Fifth Discipline: The Art and Practice of The
Learning Organisation', Random House Business Books.

67 Senge PM (2006). 'The Fifth Discipline: The Art and Practice of The Learning
Organisation', Random House Business Books.

68 Sahlberg P (2021). 'Finnish Lessons 3.0: What Can the World Learn from
Educational Change in Finland', Teachers College Press.

69 Brown B (2018). 'Dare to Lead: Brave Work, Tough Conversations, Whole
Hearts', Penguin Random House UK.

70 Senge PM (2006). 'The Fifth Discipline: The Art and Practice of The Learning
Organisation', Random House Business Books.

71 Senge PM (2006, p. 61). 'The Fifth Discipline: The Art and Practice of The
Learning Organisation', Random House Business Books.

12 Leadership Learnings

The subject of educational leadership continues to generate consider-able interest and debate resulting in a plethora of diverse concepts and models perceived through a range of perspectives.[1,2,3] Categorising such wide ranging studies in a variable and unstable field is challenging, with purpose, personality and process often confusingly interwoven.[4] Ambiguity is increased further by the assessment of formal leadership based largely on *indirect* measures with whole school responsibilities impacting student learning through multiple fields.[5] Leadership is a un-doubtedly a complex skillset which requires the development of effective practice given that the quality of leadership in schools has been consist-ently found to be a key determinant of educational outcomes.[6,7,8] Moreo-ver, schools are naturally hierarchical organisations where leadership is both formal and informal, and although formal leadership is typically the focus of educational change and improvement studies, the status of teachers as leaders is also widely recognised.[9] Undoubtedly, every stage of my educational journey has required developing leadership skills, as a leader of students, colleagues, departments and schools. Leadership for learning is arguably an undertaking which concerns all school staff, and when dispersed widely across school communities, it has the potential to maximise desirable educational outcomes for all students.[10]

Defining Educational Leadership

Definitions of leadership generally include the notion of *influence*, plac-ing focus on interactions or actions of some kind which motivate others towards the achievement of desired goals.[11] However, the way in which *power* operates within influencing activities is a key consideration for educators who work in a context where status differentials and hierarchi-cal structures exacerbate the risks associated with power. 'School leaders have enormous power and influence, and how they use that power and influence changes people. For better or worse'.[12] The use of power is not only foundational to understanding leadership practice[13] but is also

DOI: 10.4324/9781003466963-14

linked with responsibility. The greater the level of responsibility, the greater the breadth and scope for exercising power; for formal leaders, this includes promoting the conditions or managing processes through which teachers and students can be optimally effective. Equally, the scope for teachers to exercise power is wide-ranging through their professional responsibilities towards students, colleagues, the school institution and its stakeholders.[14] Although practitioners do not have equal leverage in changing school systems, the nature of social and power relations exercised by leaders at all levels points to a corresponding need for healthy use of power by all those bearing leadership responsibility in school organisations.

A sense of responsibility typically arises from commitment to a *purpose that matters* which is consistent with the ethical nature of the teaching and learning profession.[15] If leadership involves the exercise of power in influencing actions and interactions, arguably practitioners bear responsibility for the manner in which they exercise the power invested in them. Rather than holding power *over* others, responsible use of power leads to *empowering* leadership which[16]:

- Builds collective strength by sharing power *with* others.
- Recognises people's unique potential and gives them agency *to* learn and contribute.
- Develops power *within* whereby people operate with increased motivation from a place of self-worth and self-knowledge to value others and achieve purpose.

Thus, whether by selection, election or initiative, through the lens of power and responsibility, educational leadership can be defined as *assuming responsibility to empower educationally desirable outcomes by direct or indirect means*. Irrespective of practitioner status, leadership effectiveness is determined by the way power is used to empower others thereby achieving educationally desirable outcomes in classrooms, schools and the wider community.

Power and Vulnerability

Arguably, a range of organisational concerns relating to issues such as culture, change or learning and development can be more clearly understood through the lens of power. Although anomalies of structure or policy require attention, within schools problems tend to arise in the way people think, make decisions and interact.[17] Moreover, the consequences of actions extend beyond the boundaries of position impacting more widely within organisations, so understanding the nature of power and barriers to empowerment is essential.[18] Martin Luther King

Jr appositely defined leadership power as *the ability to achieve purpose and effect change*[19] pointing to power itself as neither inherently good nor bad; at both ends of the spectrum, power is problematic. Neither dictatorship nor powerlessness are desirable human states, and as indicated, the danger lies not in power per se, but rather in the way it is used.[20] Healthy use of power empowers others promoting purpose, confidence and change; conversely, power can be used detrimentally, stifling growth, creating insecurity and resistance.[21] Moreover, *avoiding* the exercise of power to circumvent the discomfort leadership can generate, leads fear and resentment to spiral[22]; thus, there is no evading the responsibility power affords.

Understanding the interplay between power and vulnerability is critical because if leaders are driven by unattended fears, defence mechanisms are likely to create barriers to empowerment.[23] Just as research points to the detrimental impacts of vulnerability and shame defences on student trust and learning,[24] leaders who use mechanisms to avoid or offload emotional discomfort can negatively influence their own and others' ability to achieve purpose and effect change. The level of reported incidents of workplace bullying in schools[25] arising from 'an abuse or misuse of power that undermines, humiliates, or causes physical or emotional harm'[26] signals the need to take power issues seriously. In some cases, leaders may be authentic in the sense of being true to themselves, but they may simultaneously display narcissistic or other dysfunctional personality traits linked to status and power.[27] An excessive need for compliance and control is an example of a defence mechanism typically related to fear and vulnerability which is symptomatic of holding power over others.[28] Furthermore, when promoted to senior positions, practitioners invariably confront issues more complex and diverse than their personal experience, and as previously indicated, leadership can create a misguided need to know the answers or solve the problems rather than seeking advice or help. Learning-related vulnerabilities such as exposing defective thinking, incompetence or weakness are often heightened for leaders[29] who may adopt defensive routines as a response.

The more senior the position or the greater the status differentials, the wider the repercussions of using defensive routines which sap others' energy, motivation and commitment. Moreover, when directed towards students with systemic vulnerabilities or those for whom school inclusion presents a challenge, the impact is typically more profound as their experiences are often linked with feelings of powerlessness; hence, they too become proficient in defensive routines leading to unhealthy relational cycles. The mantle of leadership thus requires caution, and a clearer understanding of its 'shadow aspects' as whilst the power it affords can be instrumental in promoting social good; equally, it can be instrumental in exacerbating social harm.[30]

Developing the courage to be vulnerable is a key undertaking for leaders because when confronted with power over approaches, 'the human spirit's instinct is to rise, resist and rebel' leading to spiralling mistrust and disengagement.[31] If leaders neglect to pay careful attention to the emotional arena when implementing change for example, it is unlikely that it will be embedded, not because people resist change itself but because they resist *being* changed.[32] In times of uncertainty, leaders are responsible for emotionally holding collective discomfort by acknowledging and normalising vulnerability rather than allowing unrest and division to fester or laying the blame elsewhere.[33] Learning to bear risk, uncertainty and emotional exposure bravely is thus foundational to empowering leadership. A headteacher once asked me to attend a meeting with a parent of a systemically vulnerable student which she accurately anticipated would be challenging. The parent became very angry, directing their anger vociferously at the headteacher and continuing to do so publicly as she left the school. In our de-brief, my concern was to ameliorate the feelings of the headteacher who was visibly shaken, but she simply turned to me and asked how she could have improved her communication – what approach could she have taken to assuage the parent's emotional distress? The headteacher's response was an unforgettable moment of humility, courage and empowerment.

Sources of Leadership Discomfort

In England, school leaders face increasing ethical dilemmas, and hard judgement calls in a context of work intensification, resource scarcity and parental expectation. Decision-makers are often presented with courses of action with uncertain outcomes which require them to choose between *least-worst* options.[34] In a pressurised system of pervasive accountability, market insecurity and competition, a climate of fear can pervade leading to unethical behaviours such as off-rolling poorly performing students in pursuit of higher performance outcomes.[35] Additionally, on a daily basis, leaders encounter sources of emotional discomfort which test their interactional choices and behaviours. In organisations around the world, commonly identified leadership challenges include[36,37]:

- Hard conversations including giving honest, productive feedback.
- Affording time to address and acknowledge fears and feelings rather than spending disproportional time managing problematic behaviours.
- Lack of connection and empathy leading to diminishing trust.
- Cultures of conformism where people are afraid to speak up, say something wrong or be wrong, leading to a dearth of creative ideas, critical thinking and innovation.

- A surfeit of shame, blame and perfectionism rather than taking responsibility and being accountable.
- Applying short-term solutions to problems rather than seeking to question, understand and address underlying patterns and causes.
- Aligning organisational values with practice using behaviour exemplars that can be taught, developed and evaluated.

As a deputy headteacher, I recall feeling acutely anxious when formally observed giving lesson observation feedback to a teacher undergoing a performance capability process who I was supporting. Prior to the feedback meeting, the teacher told me she would kill herself if the lesson had not met performance standards, and unfortunately the lesson had not. Other people's fears and anxieties can exacerbate one's own, and it requires courage to give difficult feedback in a clear and kind manner whilst maintaining emotional boundaries. The greater the level of leadership responsibility, the greater the potential for emotional discomfort and thus empowering leaders are rare, precisely because few people are willing to endure the discomfort required.[38] From communicating hard messages in a productive way to staff, parents and students, to navigating complexity, public speaking, change processes, decision-making or trust, sources of discomfort for educational leaders invariably require adept navigation of vulnerability and courage.

Mastering Fear

Firstly, it is important to recognise that fear is normal, necessary and creative; it is an elemental human alarm system which serves as a warning in the face of threats to physical or psychological well-being as well as a creative force that enables progress and innovation in the face of fears about human circumstances or conditions.[39] The majority of fears are environmentally acquired, and the problem is not how to be rid of fear but how to harness and master it, which is an enduring human challenge.[40] Psychologist colleagues identify fear as a derivative emotion which can easily be missed in presentations of secondary emotions such as anger, anxiety or depression. Feelings of shame typically cloak people's deepest fears, but fear can also arise simply from the anticipation of rekindling old shame. If humans are hard-wired for connection and belonging, the fear of disconnection and shame will always be present in people's lives.[41]

The problem with unharnessed fear is that in combination with leadership power, fears can surface unbidden, exacerbating the risk of power over behaviours and distrust.[42] Typically, in organisations people offload painful emotions to people they perceive to be lower in status, avoiding the presence of seniors or people they want to impress.[43]

In schools rated good by Ofsted, I have heard senior leaders venting at students in a frightening manner in the privacy of their offices or sometimes in public spaces; invariably, the students at the receiving end are systemically vulnerable and disempowered. On one occasion, concerned about the impact on a particular student, I checked in and asked if he was alright. 'Yes Miss' he replied, 'it's OK, I'm used to it.' If offloading painful emotions becomes a cultural norm, then shame will undoubtedly spread – behind classroom doors, in corridors, offices, staffrooms and amongst the student population. The complication is that people who experience feelings of powerlessness or shame on the receiving end of unharnessed fear typically repeat similar behaviour patterns if they themselves are in positions of power.[44]

Human experience is full of secret fears, some of which turn out to be more imaginary than real when uncovered, but whether rooted in childhood experiences, sense of inferiority or misplaced pride, the first step in mastering fear is to gain understanding about its *source* and *nature*:

> First we must unflinchingly face our fears and honestly ask ourselves why we are afraid. This confrontation will, to some measure, grant us power. We shall never be cured of fear by escapism or repression, for the more we attempt to ignore and repress our fears, the more we multiply our inner conflicts.[45]

Mastering fear requires a commitment to social and emotional learning because humans are emotional, interdependent beings who benefit from understanding emotional messages and engaging in the discipline of emotional learning which is a key aspect of personal development. Given that emotional development is not pursued with the same determination as physical or intellectual development,[46] arguably it is unsurprising that emotional health is identified as increasingly problematic and in decline. However, there is a call for greater attention to be given to individual leaders' personal development[47] which is a necessary step towards empowering leadership, although it must be recognised that it is not a practice which can be foisted on others.[48]

Initiatives to promote personal development in organisations are encouraging, however. In British Columbia, an Interior Health authority struggling to attract and retain engaged employees established a *Leader Within* program to encourage and support the personal development of all staff. Early results of the pilot project pointed to the promise of profound cultural change within the health authority.[49] In Singapore, a study of school principals undertaking personal mastery training[50] found that self-reflexivity – a process involving engagement with the inner self – was a key factor contributing to leaders' ability to meet highly demanding roles; furthermore, these leaders advocated for expanding personal growth training to all practitioners.[51] In England, the benefits of emotional literacy development through the social and emotional aspects of learning (SEAL) curriculum were widely recognised with improvements in student learning, behaviour and whole school culture evident.[52] The abolition of the SEAL initiative prior to its roll out in secondary schools was arguably regrettable, given its reported effectiveness. However, until such time as there is renewed legitimacy for emotion-based learning in schools, *modelling* is proffered as the most effective strategy to encourage people on their inner journeys: 'There's nothing more powerful you can do to encourage others in their quest for personal mastery than to be serious in your own quest'.[53]

Developing Courage

As indicated, the ability to successfully navigate vulnerability requires courage; it requires courage to harness fear, risk failure, challenge the status quo, engage in hard conversations or stand up and be accountable. 'The brave man is not he who does not feel afraid, but he who conquers that fear'.[54] The meaning of courage here is not in the sense of heroic deeds but rather a determination of mind – an inner resolve to face fear, bear the discomfort, move forward and refuse to be overwhelmed by it.[55] Mandela for example attests that he felt fear more times than he could remember, but he hid it behind 'a mask of boldness'.[56] Decades of leadership wisdom point to harnessing fear and embracing vulnerability as essential building blocks of courage.[57,58] It is salient that contemporary medical researchers in the field of psychology are investigating the concept of courage to advance treatments for anxiety and develop behavioural understanding.[59] Courageous action arises from fear that is acknowledged, felt and overcome in times of challenge and vulnerability. Moreover, the courage to bear vulnerability is advantageous in other ways; it gives rise to curiosity and personal learning, enables the ability to navigate complexity or paradoxical tension and promotes the development of a disciplined, intelligent mind.[60]

> One day we will learn that the heart can never be totally right if the head is totally wrong. Only through the bringing together of head and heart – intelligence and goodness – shall man rise to fulfilment of his true nature.[61]

It is salient that the *intelligence* referred to in this quote neither arises from nor is dependent upon academic prowess. Rather, it is an intrapersonal intelligence arising from 'open mindedness, sound judgment and love for truth', a type of human intelligence which is arguably impoverished due to a universal tendency to seek easy answers and short-term solutions rather than disciplining the mind to engage in contemplative, reflective thinking.[62] Open-mindedness, sound judgement and love for truth are not simply dispositional but develop as a result of disciplined practice:

- *Open-mindedness* requires the discipline to listen but also importantly to reflect – to look inward and become more aware of 'the biases and limitations in our own thinking'.[63] Otherwise, sincere ignorance and conscientious stupidity can become dangerous forces which trap people into defensive patterns of thinking and acting.[64]
- *Sound judgement* develops from taking the stance of the learner and evaluating the facts from a range of perspectives. Research shows that the human brain tends to seek predictable storytelling, causing people to confabulate endings and replace missing information with what they believe to be true.[65] In contrast, sound judgement requires the forbearance to question and evaluate the evidence before reaching conclusions.[66]
- *Love for truth* requires the practice of self-examining deep-seated beliefs or mental models of how the world works which are rarely based on truth, but rather on assumptions and incomplete truths[67]; love for truth involves holding firm to purpose whilst letting go of the need for certainty and being prepared to continually reconsider beliefs and accepted theories.[68]

Thus, courage develops through mastery of a combination of intelligences relating to both the emotions and the mind: tough-minded and tender-hearted, strong back and soft front, head and heart are examples of language used to describe the attributes of courageous leaders who empower others. Without a vulnerable heart rooted in *love*, there is a danger of leaders rising to the 'disciplined heights of toughmindedness' but simultaneously sinking to the 'passionless depths of hardheartedness'.[69] Proffered as the 'most durable power in the world'[70] through which the power to achieve purpose and effect change is made manifest, there is a price to pay for love because:

> To love is to be vulnerable. Love anything and your heart will certainly be wrung and possibly broken. If you want to make sure of keeping it intact, you must give it to no one, not even an animal … Lock it up safe in the casket or coffin of your selfishness. But in that casket, safe, dark, motionless, airless, it will change. It will not be broken; it will become unbreakable, impenetrable, irredeemable.[71]

Pedagogical love or passion (originating from the Greek word *pathos* meaning to suffer) arguably encapsulates the expression of love which lies at the heart of empowering educational leadership. Passion is tendered as the driving force required for the fulfilment of human purpose,[72] and as Finnish educators contend, love expressed through deep ethical care and trust in students cannot be ignored when reflecting on good teacherhood.[73] Courageous leaders who harness fear, discipline the mind and risk love for the sake of a noble educational purpose empower others because as they let their own lights shine, they unconsciously give other people permission to do the same; as people are liberated from their own fear, their presence automatically liberates others.[74] Robinson recounts the story of his father who although rendered paraplegic following an horrific accident at work, lived for another 18 purposeful years – double the known lifespan for paraplegia; 'The power within him,' Robinson testifies, 'inspired everybody else who met him'.[75]

Although there are no 'hard and fast absolutes' in the field of social science, 'there are truths about shared experiences that deeply resonate with what we believe and know'.[76] As a senior leader in a school where the leadership practice was deeply concerning, I was confronted with seemingly insurmountable barriers, and experienced adversity and failure along the way; the physics of vulnerability means that people who take up a call to courage will sometimes fall.[77] Over the course of a lengthy and challenging process, there was not a moment when I felt brave and recognition of the experience as courage-building came only later. Arguably, courageous action does not *feel* courageous at the time; it is always a hard call that can best be met through holding firm to purpose, building sufficient skills and reaching out to people we trust. Advantageously research points to courage as transformative, changing the structure of the emotions, so there is no going back to the place we were before which is a truth that resonates for me.[78] Regrettably, in this case, there were casualties along the way, and I was deeply shocked to hear that a student who had been the recipient of power misuse took his life shortly after leaving the school. Although circumstances render it impossible to substantiate a causal link, arguably it is not possible to underestimate the power and attendant responsibility invested in leaders to emotionally safeguard both practitioners and young people in schools.

Team Learning

The intensification of workload in schools has resulted in the need for *distributed* or *collaborative* leadership as opposed to traditional models of the solo or heroic leader.[79] Whilst there is ongoing debate about the form of leadership distribution, whether it tends more towards interaction and collaboration or delegation,[80] leadership teams in schools have become the norm. Whilst all leaders assume responsibilities, those carrying the greatest level of responsibility have a significant role in building commitment and capacity for organisations to learn at all levels.[81] Headteachers, principals or trust CEOs typically assume the greatest responsibility, relying on consistent application and approaches by their senior and middle leadership teams. Heads and leadership teams thus play a pivotal role in modelling and promoting collaborative ways of working and learning that are reciprocated within the school community. However, an identified problem for leadership teams is that they are susceptible to an apparent learning disability as illustrated by a team of committed leaders with *individual* intelligence quotients (IQ) above 120 but a *collective* IQ of only 63.[82] This apparent learning disability has consequences if unrecognised and requires leaders to grasp that team learning is a *team* skill and thus learning teams need to learn how to *learn together*:

> Team learning is vital because teams, not individuals, are the fundamental learning unit in modern organisations…; unless teams can learn, the organisation cannot learn.[83]

Given the interrelationship between vulnerability, relational trust and empowering leadership, it is unsurprising that research points to relational trust as a strong determinant of organisational success across multiple domains including leadership teams, community cohesion, culture and change processes.[84] Relational trust is vital to achieve the alignment necessary to promote an environment where collectively teams can be more insightful and effective than their individual members can be.[85] Furthermore, cultures built on care, connection, empathy and trustworthy practice promote optimum conditions for the skills underlying empowering leadership teams to flourish. Although there are a myriad of priorities for school leaders, without operationalising trust, collective learning and empowerment will be compromised by defensive routines in response to vulnerability: 'We ignore trust issues at the expense of our own performance, and the expense of our team's and organisation's success'.[86] The tougher the decisions being taken, the greater the stakes because behind the closed doors of senior leadership meetings, the fear of being judged or misunderstood, feeling stupid, making mistakes or experiencing shame are significant. Habitually resorting to defensive routines leads to unhealthy cultures of conformism where 'people fear nothing more terribly than to take a position which stands out sharply and clearly from the prevailing opinion'[87]; thus, courage, collective learning and empowerment are compromised.

As indicated, the greater the level of leadership responsibility, the greater the potential for emotional discomfort and the capacity for empowering leadership can never be greater than leaders' collective capacity for vulnerability.[88] Building relational trust enables team members to feel sufficiently safe to engage in open, sometimes uncomfortable *dialogue* to learn and participate in meetings. Typically, when differences of opinion arise, individual views based on underlying assumptions are often presented and defended with the intention of persuading others or winning an argument whilst others remain silent. Although this *discussion* type communication may be necessary when decisions have to be made, team learning through *dialogue* rests on ideas *flowing freely*. Collective participation is necessary whereby conflicting views and underlying assumptions are surfaced uncritically, generating shared understandings and innovative solutions drawn from a 'pool of common meaning' which cannot be accessed individually.[89] A level playing field devoid of hierarchical power and deep trust are needed to engage in empowering dialogue of this nature.[90]

Furthermore, when operating from fear or emotions which drive self-protection, people predictably move from a mindset of self-deprecation to arrogance whereby *the ego* takes control.[91] The ego can be healthy or unhealthy, and effective ego management is important because the power afforded to leaders can increase the risk of unhealthy ego management. The ego seeks acceptance and approval, so vulnerability poses too great a risk in situations where being liked or respected is at risk.[92] Fortunately, the ego is just a small part of who people are in comparison to the heart which is huge and well equipped to still the inner voice of the ego if it remains vulnerable and open.[93] Learning teams must be committed to both acknowledging the truth of what's going on 'out there' in the reality of their organisation, but also about 'what's going on "in here" within the team itself'.[94] Without the capacity for vulnerability, collective power is untethered and steered by unhealthy drivers leading to organisational stagnation and distrust. Conversely, collective ability to achieve purpose and effect change resides in vulnerability – the seat of difficult emotions but also the seat of human thriving; a humanising and creative attribute that enables empowerment.

Arguably, effective educational leadership is not accurately determined by the outcomes of the most able or stable students but rather by how those bearing systemic vulnerabilities are included and fare in England's education system. Experience points to the existence of empowering school leaders who change lives, but there remains considerable work to do. This will necessitate school leaders working collectively to disperse understanding and champion informed practice to foster practitioners who:

- understand the cost of unaddressed fears and bias
- question assumptions and reconfigure narrow perceptions of intelligence and curriculums

- re-examine internally held models and beliefs about how education systems work
- engage individually and collectively in disciplined and courageous practice
- maximise educationally desirable outcomes for all students

When the time comes that educational governance and leadership are aligned and operationalising relational trust is the *modus operandi* in every school (Appendix J), arguably organisational empowerment will retain and engage creative, committed and purposeful practitioners who transform education systems and outcomes for all students; meanwhile, perseverance, courage and vision are needed.

Worthwhile change requires a perception that schools must be different because the world must be different and a recognition that schools can and must contribute to this wider change.[95]

Notes

1 West-Burnham J (2009). 'Leadership for Transformation', Rethinking Educational Leadership: From Improvement to Transformation, pp. 7–23, Continuum.
2 Wilson M (2014). 'Critical Reflection on Authentic Leadership and School Leader Development from a Virtue Ethical Perspective', *Educational Review*, Vol. 66, No. 4, pp. 482–496, https://doi.org/10.1080/00131911.2013.812062.
3 Connolly M, James C & Fertig M (2019). 'The Difference between Educational Management and Educational Leadership and the Importance of Educational Responsibility', *Educational Management Administration & Leadership*, Vol. 47, No. 4, pp. 504–519, https://doi.org/10.1177/1741143217745880.
4 Lingard B, Hays D, Mills M & Christie P (2003). 'Leading Theory', Leading Learning: Making Hope Practical in Schools, pp. 51–78, Open University Press.
5 Ofsted (2019). 'Education Inspection Framework: Overview of Research', Ref No. 180045.
6 Cranston N (2013). 'School Leaders Leading: Professional Responsibility Not Accountability as the Key Focus', *Educational Management, Administration & Leadership*, Vol. 41, No. 2, pp. 129–142, https://doi.org/10.1177/1741143212468348.
7 Ofsted (2019). 'Education Inspection Framework: Overview of Research', Ref No. 180045.
8 Earley P (2020). 'Surviving, Thriving and Reviving in Leadership: The Personal and Professional Development Needs of Educational Leaders', *Management in Education*, Vol. 34, No. 3, pp. 117–121, https://doi.org/10.1177/0892020620919763.
9 Sahlberg P (2021). 'Finnish Lessons 3.0', Teachers College Press.
10 Lingard B, Hays D, Mills M & Christie P (2003). 'Leading Theory', Leading Learning: Making Hope Practical in Schools, pp. 51–78, Open University Press.
11 Connolly M, James C & Fertig M (2019). 'The Difference between Educational Management and Educational Leadership and the Importance of Educational

a

Responsibility', *Educational Management Administration & Leadership*, Vol. 47, No. 4, pp. 504–519, https://doi.org/10.1177/1741143217745880.
12 Brown B (2018, p. 132). 'Dare to Lead: Brave Work, Tough Conversations, Whole Hearts', Penguin Random House UK.
13 Brown B (2020). 'Dare to Lead' at brenebrown.com/daretolead, https://brenebrown.com/hubs/dare-to-lead/. Accessed 01.07.24.
14 Connolly M, James C & Fertig M (2019). 'The Difference between Educational Management and Educational Leadership and the Importance of Educational Responsibility', *Educational Management Administration & Leadership*, Vol. 47, No. 4, pp. 504–519, https://doi.org/10.1177/1741143217745880.
15 Connolly M, James C & Fertig M (2019). 'The Difference between Educational Management and Educational Leadership and the Importance of Educational Responsibility', *Educational Management Administration & Leadership*, Vol. 47, No. 4, pp. 504–519, https://doi.org/10.1177/1741143217745880.
16 Brown B (2020). 'Dare to Lead' at brenebrown.com/daretolead, https://brenebrown.com/hubs/dare-to-lead/. Accessed 01.07.24.
17 Senge PM (2006). 'The Fifth Discipline: The Art & Practice of the Learning Organisation', Random House Business Books.
18 Senge PM (2006). 'The Fifth Discipline: The Art & Practice of the Learning Organisation', Random House Business Books.
19 King ML, Jr (1963). 'A Gift of Love', Penguin Random House UK.
20 Brown B (2020). 'Dare to Lead' at brenebrown.com/daretolead, file:https://brenebrown.com/hubs/dare-to-lead/. Accessed 01.07.24.
21 Holmes K, Clement J & Albright J (2013). 'The Complex Task of Leading Educational Change in Schools', *School Leadership and Management*, Vol. 33, No. 3, pp. 270–283.
22 Shortland ND, McCusker ME, Alison L, Blacksmith N, Crayne MP, Thompson L, Gonzales J, McGarry P & Stevens C (2022). 'Avoidant Authority: The Effect of Organisational Power on Decision-Making in High-Uncertainty Situations', *Frontiers in Psychology*, Vol. 13, 1027108, https://doi.org/10.3389/fpsyg.2022.1027108.
23 King ML, Jr (1963). 'A Gift of Love', Penguin Random House UK.
24 Byrnell VH (2019). 'Academic Paper and Conference Presentation', St Mary's University.
25 Education Support (2024). 'Bullying and Harassment', https://www.educationsupport.org.uk/resources/for-individuals/guides/bullying-and-harassment/. Accessed 10.07.24.
26 ACAS (2023, npr). 'Bullying at Work', https://www.acas.org.uk/bullying-at-work#:~:text=Examples%20of%20bullying&text=constantly%20putting%20someone%20down%20in,or%20photos%20on%20social%20media. Accessed 10.07.24.
27 Wilson M (2014). 'Critical Reflection on Authentic Leadership and School Leader Development from a Virtue Ethical Perspective', *Educational Review*, Vol. 66, No. 4, pp. 482–496, https://doi.org/10.1080/00131911.2013.812062.
28 Brown B (2018). 'Dare to Lead: Brave Work, Tough Conversations, Whole Hearts', Penguin Random House UK.
29 Senge PM (2006). 'The Fifth Discipline: The Art & Practice of the Learning Organisation', Random House Business Books.
30 Lingard B, Hays D, Mills M & Christie P (2003). 'Leading Theory', Leading Learning: Making Hope Practical in Schools, pp. 51–78, Open University Press.
31 Brown B (2018, p. 96). 'Dare to Lead: Brave Work, Tough Conversations, Whole Hearts', Penguin Random House UK.

32 Senge PM (2006). 'The Fifth Discipline: The Art & Practice of the Learning Organisation', Random House Business Books.
33 Brown B (2018). 'Dare to Lead: Brave Work, Tough Conversations, Whole Hearts', Penguin Random House UK.
34 Shortland ND, McCusker ME, Alison L, Blacksmith N, Crayne MP, Thompson L, Gonzales J, McGarry P & Stevens C (2022). 'Avoidant Authority: The Effect of Organisational Power on Decision-Making in High-Uncertainty Situations', *Frontiers in Psychology*, Vol. 13, 1027108, https://doi.org/10.3389/fpsyg.2022.1027108.
35 BELMAS (2020, p. 32). 'Educational Leadership, Management and Administration in the United Kingdom: A Comparative Review', Project reporters: Woods PA, Simkins T, Donnelly C, Hamilton T, Jones K, Potter I, Torrance D.
36 Senge PM (2006). 'The Fifth Discipline: The Art & Practice of the Learning Organisation', Random House Business Books.
37 Brown B (2018). 'Dare to Lead: Brave Work, Tough Conversations, Whole Hearts', Penguin Random House UK.
38 Brown B (2013). 'Daring Greatly: How the Courage to be Vulnerable Transforms the Way We Live, Love, Parent and Lead', Penguin Random House UK.
39 King ML, Jr (1963). 'A Gift of Love', Penguin Random House UK.
40 King ML, Jr (1963). 'A Gift of Love', Penguin Random House UK.
41 Brown B (2018). 'Dare to Lead: Brave Work, Tough Conversations, Whole Hearts', Penguin Random House UK.
42 Brown B (2018). 'Dare to Lead: Brave Work, Tough Conversations, Whole Hearts', Penguin Random House UK.
43 Brown B (2018). 'Dare to Lead: Brave Work, Tough Conversations, Whole Hearts', Penguin Random House UK.
44 Brown B (2018). 'Dare to Lead: Brave Work, Tough Conversations, Whole Hearts', Penguin Random House UK.
45 King ML, Jr (1963, p. 116). 'A Gift of Love', Penguin Random House UK.
46 Senge PM (2006, p. 133, citing O'Brien W, 2006). 'The Fifth Discipline: The Art & Practice of the Learning Organisation', Random House Business Books.
47 Earley P (2020). 'Surviving, Thriving and Reviving in Leadership: The Personal and Professional Development Needs of Educational Leaders', *Management in Education*, Vol. 34, No. 3, pp. 117–121, https://doi.org/10.1177/0892020620919763.
48 Senge PM (2006). 'The Fifth Discipline: The Art & Practice of the Learning Organisation', Random House Business Books.
49 Koehle M, Bird D & Bonney C (2008). 'The Role of Personal Mastery in Clinical Practice: How Personal Leadership Can Transform the Workplace', *Journal of PeriAnesthesia Nursing*, Vol. 23, No. 3, pp. 172–182, https://www.sciencedirect.com/science/article/abs/pii/S1089947208000646.
50 Senge PM (2006). 'The Fifth Discipline: The Art & Practice of the Learning Organisation', Random House Business Books.
51 Retna KS (2011). 'The Relevance of 'Personal Mastery' to Leadership: The Case of School Principals in Singapore', *School Leadership and Management*, Vol. 31, No. 5, pp. 451–470.
52 Hallam S (2009). 'An Evaluation of the Social and Emotional Aspects of Learning (SEAL) Programme: Promoting Positive Behaviour, Effective Learning and Well-Being in Primary School Children', *Oxford Review of Education*, Vol. 35, No. 3, pp. 313–330, https://www.tandfonline.com/doi/epdf/10.1080/03054980902934597?needAccess=true.
53 Senge PM (2006, p. 162). 'The Fifth Discipline: The Art & Practice of the Learning Organisation', Random House Business Books.

54 Mandela N (1994, p. 615). 'Long Walk to Freedom', Macdonald Purnell (PTY) Ltd.
55 King ML, Jr (1963). 'A Gift of Love', Penguin Random House UK.
56 Mandela N (1994, p. 615). 'Long Walk to Freedom', Macdonald Purnell (PTY) Ltd.
57 King ML, Jr (1963). 'A Gift of Love', Penguin Random House UK.
58 Mandela N (1994). 'Long Walk to Freedom', Macdonald Purnell (PTY) Ltd.
59 Norton PJ & Weiss BJ (2009). 'The Role of Courage on Behavioural Approach in a Fear-Eliciting Situation: A Proof-of-Concept Pilot Study', *National Institutes of Health*, Vol. 23, No. 2, pp. 212–217, https://doi.org/10.1016/j.janxdis.2008.07.002.
60 Brown B (2018). 'Dare to Lead: Brave Work, Tough Conversations, Whole Hearts', Penguin Random House UK.
61 King ML, Jr (1963, p. 43). 'A Gift of Love', Penguin Random House UK.
62 King ML, Jr (1963, p. 43). 'A Gift of Love', Penguin Random House UK.
63 Senge PM (2006, p. 261). 'The Fifth Discipline: The Art & Practice of the Learning Organisation', Random House Business Books.
64 King ML, Jr (1963). 'A Gift of Love', Penguin Random House UK.
65 Brown B (2015, p. 4). 'Rising Strong: If We Are Brave Enough, Often Enough, We Will Fall', Penguin Random House UK.
66 King ML, Jr (1963). 'A Gift of Love', Penguin Random House UK.
67 Senge PM (2006). 'The Fifth Discipline: The Art & Practice of the Learning Organisation', Random House Business Books.
68 Senge PM (2006). 'The Fifth Discipline: The Art & Practice of the Learning Organisation', Random House Business Books.
69 King ML, Jr (1963, p. 6). 'A Gift of Love', Penguin Random House UK.
70 King ML, Jr (1963, p. 54). 'A Gift of Love', Penguin Random House UK.
71 Lewis CS (1960, p. 111). 'The Four Loves', Harper Collins.
72 Robinson K (2015). 'Finding Your Element' King Roase Archives, https://www.youtube.com/watch?v=17fbxRQgMlU. Accessed 26.07.24.
73 Maatta K & Uusiautti S (2011). 'Pedagogical Love and Good Teacherhood', https://www.researchgate.net/publication/351141815_Pedagogical_Love_and_Good_Teacherhood. Accessed 16.05.22.
74 Williamson M (1996). 'A Return to Love: Reflections on the Principles of a Course in Miracles', Thorsons.
75 Robinson K (2015). 'Finding Your Element' King Roase Archives, https://www.youtube.com/watch?v=17fbxRQgMlU. Accessed 26.07.24.
76 Brown B (2015, p. 4). 'Rising Strong: If We Are Brave Enough, Often Enough, We Will Fall', Penguin Random House UK.
77 Brown B (2015). 'Rising Strong: If We Are Brave Enough, Often Enough, We Will Fall', Penguin Random House UK.
78 Brown B (2015). 'Rising Strong: If We Are Brave Enough, Often Enough, We Will Fall', Penguin Random House UK.
79 Harris A (2013). 'Distributed Leadership: Friend or Foe?', *Educational Management Administration & Leadership*, Vol. 41, No. 5, pp. 545–554, https://doi.org/10.1177/1741143213497635.
80 Lahtero TJ, Ahtiaines RS & Lang N (2019). 'Finnish Principals: Leadership Training and Views on Distributed Leadership', *Academic Journals*, Vol. 14, No. 10, pp. 340–348, https://doi.org/10.5897/ERR2018.3637.
81 Senge PM (2006). 'The Fifth Discipline: The Art & Practice of the Learning Organisation', Random House Business Books.
82 Senge PM (2006). 'The Fifth Discipline: The Art & Practice of the Learning Organisation', Random House Business Books.

83 Senge PM (2006, p. 10). 'The Fifth Discipline: The Art & Practice of the Learning Organisation', Random House Business Books.

84 Cerna L (2014). 'Trust: What It Is and Why It Matters for Governance and Education', OECD Educational Working Paper No 108, https://www.oecd-ilibrary.org/education/trust-what-it-is-and-why-it-matters-for-governance-and-education_5jxswcg0t6wl-en.

85 Senge PM (2006). 'The Fifth Discipline: The Art & Practice of the Learning Organisation', Random House Business Books.

86 Brown B (2018, p. 222). 'Dare to Lead: Brave Work, Tough Conversations, Whole Hearts', Penguin Random House UK.

87 King ML Jr, (1963, p. 14). 'A Gift of Love', Penguin Random House UK.

88 Brown B (2018). 'Dare to Lead: Brave Work, Tough Conversations, Whole Hearts', Penguin Random House UK.

89 Senge PM (2006, p. 225). 'The Fifth Discipline: The Art & Practice of the Learning Organisation', Random House Business Books.

90 Senge PM (2006). 'The Fifth Discipline: The Art & Practice of the Learning Organisation', Random House Business Books.

91 Brown B (2018). 'Dare to Lead: Brave Work, Tough Conversations, Whole Hearts', Penguin Random House UK.

92 Brown B (2018). 'Dare to Lead: Brave Work, Tough Conversations, Whole Hearts', Penguin Random House UK.

93 Brown B (2018). 'Dare to Lead: Brave Work, Tough Conversations, Whole Hearts', Penguin Random House UK.

94 Senge PM (2006, p. 240). 'The Fifth Discipline: The Art & Practice of the Learning Organisation', Random House Business Books.

95 Wrigley T, Lingard B & Thomson P (2012, p. 101). 'Pedagogies of Transformation: Keeping Hope Alive in Troubled Times', *Critical Studies in Education*, Vol. 51, No. 1, pp. 95–108, https://doi.org/10.1080/17508487.2011.637570.

13 Leading Inclusion

Setting the Scene

Inclusion is an aspect of educational leadership and governance which arguably requires more insight and strategy than has hitherto been the case as it concerns all students to a greater or lesser extent.[1] Without sufficient attention, inclusivity is at risk of remaining an aspiration, with system stressors exacerbating the impacts of underlying exclusionary structures and thinking reflected in practice. At policy level, inclusion is problematised by long-established *exclusion* processes which are an integral part of inclusion processes, and thus, inclusion and exclusion are intractably associated by definition.[2] Consequently, schools accept and even embrace exclusion as a tolerable, sometimes intentional end point for students deemed beyond help.[3] A range of metrics show that systemically vulnerable students with identifiable characteristics remain at significantly greater risk of exclusion than others[4]; additionally, there has been a rise in self-exclusion indicated by the growing number of students recorded as missing education and in home education as a last resort for parents of SEND students.[5] Although research identifies a clear relationship between school exclusion and a range of highly detrimental life outcomes, there has been a lack of questioning by policymakers into how and why identified groups of students continue to be disproportionately excluded from school.[6] Failure to understand and address factors which exacerbate exclusivity increases the risk of curtailing educational integrity, leading to unhealthy tensions between ingrained exclusionary practice and the rhetoric of school inclusion reflected in policy goals such as Educational Excellence Everywhere[7] and Opportunity for All.[8]

Extensive evidence gathered by former Children's Commissioner, Aynsley-Green, points to a deplorable track record of exclusionary attitudes towards children in England, particularly those experiencing adversity who are most in need of professional care, compassion

DOI: 10.4324/9781003466963-15

and support.[9] Inequity and exclusionary practice remain a concerning trend in a fragmented education system where systemically vulnerable young people are 'often lost to view for being the responsible people and citizens they are'.[10] Systemic vulnerabilities invariably exist in all human populations; experience points to individuals of every neurological type and difference scattered within the human spectrum, yet the issue of educational health and care plans (EHCP) in England has increased by 140% in 10 years.[11] The current level of uptake and demand for specialist school provision is both financially unsustainable and an ineffective alternative to inclusive mainstream schooling, yielding no improvement in attainment for SEND students.[12] One of a number of factors which arguably need urgent redress is the capacity of special educational needs coordinators (SENDCos) in mainstream schools. Currently, the SENDCo has central responsibility for the operation and co-ordination of provision to ensure *every learner feels included*, and for ensuring *all practitioners in the school* understand *their* responsibilities to SEND students and the school's approach to identifying and meeting their needs.[13] SENDCos are rarely senior leaders; their time is typically curtailed by teaching commitments and an inordinately high administrative load, with insufficient capacity to identify or address the needs of many of the students, let alone lead on whole school initiatives.[14]

Secondary school students are at the greatest risk of both underachievement and exclusion with persistent disruptive behaviour accounting for 48% of all reasons given for fixed-term and 39% of reasons for permanent exclusions.[15] Inequitable attainment and high exclusion rates for identified minority groups are also exacerbated by regional divisions relating to socioeconomic and resource factors in England. The correlation between eligibility for free school meals and higher exclusion rates underscores the presence of socioeconomic disparities affecting educational experiences.[16] However, addressing societal inequalities which contribute to educational inequality is plainly outside the scope of educators alone.[17] Sufficient and equitable resourcing and improvements across a range of children's services such as early years, welfare, health, youth offending and employment are also needed.[18] Nevertheless, 'teachers are second only to parents for having the greatest influence on the lives and outcomes of children'.[19] Thus, it is arguably incumbent on educational leaders to challenge exclusionary factors at school and policy level and implement strategies within their control. In the existing climate of inequality and resource scarcity, it is imperative that timely and cost-effective efforts are made to reverse the exclusionary trend, and evidencing existing good practice is a recognised step towards discourse, understanding and change.[20]

Case Study School

A pertinent case study is a state-maintained secondary school with a higher than average cohort of systemically vulnerable students in all identified at-risk groups: socio-economically disadvantaged, SEND (particularly social, emotional and mental health [SEMH]), ethnic minority groups (particularly Black and mixed-race Caribbean) and Gypsy.[21] Judged as requiring improvement in every category and with a substantial budget deficit necessitating support staff cuts, the newly appointed headteacher placed strategic focus on inclusion and aspiration across all school systems. Over the course of the first year, role restructuring ensured that all senior leaders were aligned in respect of their 'commitment to inclusive values and their capacity to lead in a participatory manner'.[22] While fixed-term exclusions remained a concern for the 25% SEND cohort, overall exclusion rates reduced, and within 18 months, Ofsted reported that under the headteachers' inspirational leadership:

- all students feel happy, welcome and safe
- students show respect and understanding towards others of different faiths, cultures and backgrounds
- students respond well to teachers because they establish positive relationships with them
- increasingly teachers plan lessons which take consideration of students' barriers to learning
- as a result of the emphasis given to preparing activities that respond to the needs of all students they make good progress from different starting points
- students communicate confidently and put effort into completing their work
- SEND provision is good and SEND students' progress is improving
- the progress of disadvantaged students is improving
- behaviour is good – a marked improvement confirmed by parents and staff
- bullying is rare, and when it happens, teachers deal with it swiftly
- many of the small number of students attending alternative provision are now educated full time in the school because school leaders have developed the capacity to address their needs
- the proportion of students in education, training or employment at the end of KS4 is higher than the national average
- teachers benefit from personalised professional development to improve their practice

Six months post-inspection, general certificate of education (GCSE) pass rates in English and Maths rose by 20%, and the school changed from the most undersubscribed to the most oversubscribed in the local authority. As Assistant Headteacher, Director of Inclusion and SENDCo, I can attest that leading inclusion was a genuinely collaborative, whole-school endeavour whereby the headteacher and senior leaders sought or considered an inclusive perspective which became woven into the fabric of the school. I had a key role in ongoing staff training, restructuring learning support provision and establishing whole-school processes which expedited access to education for systemically vulnerable young people. Experience drawn from the case study school, subsequent research and a career of leading inclusion in specialist and mainstream schools across primary and secondary phases point to some key areas for consideration.

Teacher Training

Although there are greater challenges in reducing achievement inequality in schools with high socioeconomic disadvantage and high proportions of ethnic minority students,[23] this is arguably an undertaking within educators' capacity to progress. All practitioners carry responsibility for enabling systemically vulnerable students working below expected levels to access learning and aspire. While learning support departments can provide valuable, targeted interventions, curriculum access is predominantly situated in classrooms where all children benefit when taught by competent, inclusive teachers.[24] Thus, it is essential that teachers are appropriately trained and understand the learning implications of a broad range of additional needs and systemic vulnerabilities in order to fulfil their responsibility for inclusion and build student trust. As indicated by student research participants, the trustworthy characteristic of *professional reliability* (Chapter 3) is demonstrated when *teachers* ensure that *work and homework are doable*; this was a critical factor which participants reiterated, explained and provided examples of, when explored further in focus group sessions.

Knowledge and understanding for inclusive teaching and learning is arguably a training requirement currently lacking in teacher training programmes which needs to be urgently addressed. A UNICEF study points to 'inadequate preparation of pre-service teachers for inclusive classrooms' which suggests that 'most in-service teachers in the same system are likely to struggle to include all learners in regular classrooms'.[25] At the case study school, the start of the school year included whole-school INSET designed to explore ideas and motivate staff towards a school vision for inclusion. Additionally, 10-minute weekly inclusion briefings in directed staff time were introduced; if staff absented themselves, the headteacher followed up. It transpired that even the SEND categories of need as outlined in the SEND code of practice 2014 (Appendix K) were unfamiliar to the majority of staff. Furthermore, teachers had inadequate knowledge and understanding about the implications for learning arising from a range of common needs including speech and language, working memory and/or processing difficulties, attachment disruption, neurodiversity and language acquisition for young people facing economic, racial or access inequalities.[26]

> Time and again I visit students who are unable to read the work in front of them, and/or unable to process the large amounts of verbal information flying their way and are doing everything in their power to avoid working.[27]

Given the likelihood of around a quarter of students in diverse mainstream secondary schools having some level of additional need (of itself an *inaccurate* indicator of cognitive ability), it is arguable that current teacher training programmes contribute to teacher inefficacy and exclusionary practice; a deficit which requires remedy at policy level.[28] When lecturing recently qualified early careers teachers embarking on a Masters module at St Mary's University, many selected the inclusion option on offer. In their feedback, students emphasised that it would have greatly benefitted them to learn about additional needs, systemic vulnerabilities and the links between learning and trust *in advance of* their teaching placements; it was clear they had a thirst for more knowledge and understanding.

Data Access

Systems for informing teachers about individual students' additional needs are arguably vital, particularly in secondary schools where a five-period day can involve teaching up to 150 students with some subjects allocated only limited taught time. Typically, information on students is collated in individual files which are impracticable and time-consuming for teachers to access for multiple students. EHCPs are lengthy documents, and recommended provisions often geared towards primary rather than secondary school settings. Information on students with complex needs without EHCPs may be lacking, either because previous school moves have precluded time to complete a statutory process (in which case schools have to start again, but not until a full year of attendance), or because some parents do not pursue a statutory process due to inaccessibility, or choice. For students requiring *SEND support* or those identified with *concerns* (the lower tiers of provision), information is often obtained through brief conversations between SENDCos or other inclusion leads via transition meetings. School files vary in their usefulness, and a proportion of students with additional needs arising from sociodemographic factors, or those who 'manage their challenges quietly, without complaint'[29] simply slip through the net altogether. In the existing system, primary standard assessment tests (SATs) data are an unreliable assessment tool given the number of students in secondary education with unidentified needs; thus, existing systems for providing relevant and up-to-date information to inform teachers' planning and promote inclusivity in secondary schools are arguably insufficient, unwieldy and inequitable. At the case study school, I introduced a system to provide teachers with access to data, communicating meaningful information on students' additional needs relevant to both learning and emotional factors as an initiative to combat exclusionary classroom practice.

Additional needs information is not to be confused with diagnosis because although this may be desirable, students cannot afford to prolong the time taken to be educationally supported. Many additional needs characteristics can be identified with appropriate screening systems in place; I was informed authoritatively by a SEND consultant years ago that this is a crucial aspect of a SENDCo's role. There already exist a range of suitable, cost-effective assessments; cognitive ability tests (CATs) are already in place (although underutilised), and working ages for reading comprehension and maths can be obtained easily using IT-based tests. SENDCos are equipped to scrutinise and interpret data and undertake a range of useful assessments (Appendix L) which can be carried out by colleagues with minimal direction required. Emotional literacy assessments are an invaluable tool for identifying students with perceptions of well-below average self-esteem indicative of students experiencing SEMH difficulties which may otherwise be missed. Similarly, the identification of working memory, processing and attention difficulties are extremely useful for teachers given their impact on learning and behaviours. There is arguably no reason to delay screening tests until secondary school transition, but until such systems are rolled out and embedded, a collective organisational effort is required. School leaders need to be on board because as indicated, many SENDCOs are already overburdened with administration and have insufficient time to lead on whole school initiatives.[30] Thereafter, maintaining and updating a data tracker system is a reasonably straightforward process given a sufficient level of administrative support.

The anonymised data tracker extract and accompanying explanations (Appendix M) provide an example of a data tracking system which was most effectively accessed by teachers at the case study school when also inputted on dropdown inclusion registers sitting alongside class registers on the existing school system. School registration systems have the capacity to make drop down registers readily available so that teachers can see inclusion data for the students in front of them in every lesson; it would benefit schools if system designers integrated standard proformas into their programs. In the case study school, inspectors comments endorse the positive impact of the data communication system pointing to the benefit of bringing data together and making it operationally useful[31] to ensure inclusion is structurally embedded in classroom practice. Access to data and ongoing training promoted enhanced teacher awareness and understanding of learning barriers, promoting the connection and empathy students need to build trust, risk learning and develop resilience. Deficit thinking whereby teachers perceive students themselves to be *disordered* in some way and lower their expectations creates barriers both in teacher-student and inter-student relationships. In contrast, data access enhances teacher efficacy, promoting both relational practice and student access to learning. An accurate picture is unlikely to be gleaned from the students themselves who may be unaware of their needs and are invariably skilled in developing strategies to avoid exposing their vulnerabilities, often with exclusive consequences.

Teaching and Learning

Alongside accessible data, inclusive teaching and learning strategies promote education systems within which 'teachers feel supported as well as challenged in relation to their responsibility to keep exploring more effective ways of facilitating the learning of all students'.[32] Although there is no definitive guidance on how teachers must 'adapt teaching to respond to the strengths and needs of all pupils' required by the DFE Teacher Standards,[33] differentiation or adaptative teaching is widely viewed as a strategy for improving student attainment which impacts positively on classroom experiences.[34] However, the concept of adaptive teaching is often misunderstood and regarded by teachers as *scaffolding* for weaker learners and merely a technique for addressing inequality in the classroom which places an undue burden on their planning.[35] In the case study school, a bespoke teaching and learning strategy was facilitated by an outside consultant designed collaboratively with school staff. The strategy prioritised clear, well-considered learning intentions which enabled students to reflect on their learning and select tasks suited to whether they felt confident, needed more practice or were not quite there yet (Learning Strategies, Appendix B). Teacher support was facilitated through a peer mentoring system led by newly appointed lead teachers guided by the consultant. When inspectors asked a group of high-achieving students when they last felt challenged in their learning, their response was *10 minutes ago*. The difference was that through consistent adaptive teaching, teachers had changed both their thinking and their aim. As demonstrated by the game of bowling, master bowlers never aim for the middle pin; to have the best chance of knocking down all the pins they aim for the outside pins, the ones that are hardest to reach.[36] Some teachers demonstrated extraordinary creativity in their practice and asking them to share ideas and examples in briefing sessions proved highly impactful, promoting collaborative professional learning. Experience suggests that teachers' energy reserves are boosted when they are learning, empowered, supported and student engagement maximised.

Curriculum

Having come through a system where improving the scope and recognition of alternative curriculums in KS4 was completely reversed, the national curriculum is another area of concern because arguably a succession of department of education ministers have been 'completely out of touch with what matters in life and how to achieve it through a balanced curriculum'.[37] For example, the increasingly narrow, academic focus of the KS4 curriculum in mainstream schools contrasts with many specialist schools where in addition to academic qualifications, alternative pathways, curricula and vocational qualifications are lauded. Moreover, whilst creative subjects have been downgraded in state-maintained schools, they are an ongoing priority in independent schools with many having world-class performance theatres.[38] The one-size-fits-all approach in state-maintained schools impacts a proportion of KS4 students for whom the national curriculum remains exclusionary, lacking in vocational, skills-based pathways and consistent with rising exclusion levels at this key stage. Although a detailed critique of curriculum reform is outside the scope of this chapter, policy initiatives to increase the participation of students in and reduce their exclusion from, curricula, cultures and communities of schools[39,40] are timely and pressing. The importance of multidisciplinary knowledge and skills such as critical thinking, problem solving and creativity is increasingly recognised along with value placed on vocational pathways which students with different kinds of competencies can access.[41]

Behaviour for Learning

Fast-track school improvement has been increasingly linked to implementing non-negotiable, zero-tolerance, no-excuses behaviour policies which have consequently come to be held in high regard.[42] However, there are a range of identified in-school challenges that frequently impede behaviour improvement including insufficient 'classroom management skills', 'unsuitably skilled staff in charge of pivotal behaviour roles' and 'remote, unavailable or over-occupied leadership'.[43] As identified in some schools, *consistency* can be used as a panacea which prohibits discretion, personalisation or reasonable adjustments which are all hallmarks of inclusivity.[44] Indeed, for neurodiverse students or those with learning difficulties, schools would have great difficulty in justifying inflexible application of sanctions 'as a proportionate means of achieving a legitimate aim'.[45] The disparity in allocation of school sanctions is well known; in every secondary school I have worked, behaviour management data shows that systemically vulnerable students are sanctioned disproportionately and repeatedly, arguably received by students as:

- the result of an offense
- more or less unpleasant
- the first step to a form of exclusion from class, learning or social opportunity
- more or less shaming

Although a number of factors can exacerbate school exclusion, no-excuses behaviour systems are problematic in addressing *persistent disruptive behaviour*, the most commonly cited reason for exclusion.[46] Naturally, there are instances where safety aspects of student behaviours justifiably warrant exclusionary sanctions, but if students come through a system which constantly punishes them, they can become immune to sanctions and the development of responsibility is often overlooked.[47] Thus, relational practice which promotes enquiring, non-judgemental, restorative approaches is all that remains in the arsenal whereby students *want* to put things right and change their behaviour for their teachers.[48] Tensions between traditional and relational behaviour management approaches point to the need for further investigation into systemic thinking and bias resulting in disproportionate experiences for increasing numbers of students within the education system.[49]

In England, Australia and the US, the disparate application of exclusionary practices is consistently linked with students who already experience economic inequality, racial inequality, learning deficits and impoverished access to educational support at home.[50] Moreover, the trend towards zero-tolerance approaches is pushing already marginalised students out of the academic environment for non-dangerous student behaviours including minor misdemeanours.[51] A SENDCo recently recounted her misgivings about the number of systemically vulnerable students with detentions backed up for weeks, contributing to their low mood and disengagement. One student, arriving at school with no tie, was duly given an automatic detention; the SENDCo happened to see him looking miserable and asked him where his tie was. 'I think it's in my bag', he responded. With her help, they found the tie at the bottom of his bag resulting in unnecessary time and effort removing the detention from the system and informing the parent. Traditional approaches to behaviour management leading to adverse and inequitable consequences point to the need to identify and change the leverage being used because 'unfortunately the more vigorously you push the familiar levers ... the more futile your efforts become'.[52]

The attitudes of key stakeholders including principals, teachers, parents and community members have been found to influence exclusionary approaches to systemically vulnerable young people.[53,54] Aspects of student identity sometimes invoke unintentional assumptions which 'heavily influence decision-making without conscious knowledge' resulting in deficit thinking, a dismissive mindset and withdrawal of academic and emotional support.[55] On a number of occasions, I have encountered discriminatory language and attitudes towards systemically vulnerable students. Privilege is an uncomfortable and courageous conversation which all leaders need to be having[56] including in the educational arena where factors such as race, class, sexual orientation, physical and cognitive ability are intertwined with inequity. Educational leaders need to stay curious about their own blind spots and be committed to helping colleagues identify theirs in a safe and supportive way.[57] Moreover, as participants indicated, *over-use* of sanctions is a symptom of power misuse which when normalised and modelled in schools can arguably perpetuate pervasive bias towards people experiencing disadvantage or adversity. 'To change the behaviour of the system, you must identify and change the limiting factor[s]'[58]; implicit bias is arguably a limiting factor that needs to be addressed to prevent school experiences which compound adversity with adversity, with discipline over-use and exclusion.[59,60,61] Otherwise, identified negative impacts on relational stability, belonging, mental health, access to employment and criminality, associated with high societal cost implications, are an inevitable outcome.[62]

I was told a memorable story about a university lecturer who prepared his early career teacher students for an assessment which was to be invigilated by an external assessor. The students sat in silence as the papers were handed out and began their assessment. Initially, they remained silent, but after a while, they began to fidget, chairs tipping back, tapping pens, making eye contact and trying to distract each other. Despite re-direction from the invigilator, their behaviour escalated, some talked and got out of their seats, some screwed up their papers and threw them; the room became increasingly chaotic. The lecturer then entered and explained the experiential learning session he had prepared for his students. The invigilator was in fact his well-briefed wife, and the paper he had prepared contained questions which he knew the students would find virtually impossible to answer. Almost without exception, these early careers teachers had exhibited examples of disruptive behaviours they could expect to see as a result of inaccessible learning.

Improving access to learning and relational trust practice are arguably high leverage strategies for inclusive behaviour management. In the case study school, access to learning was prioritised before inviting a working party of practitioners to design a new behaviour system. The new system had been in place for only a short period of time, yet the remarkable improvement in overall behaviour was endorsed by inspectors, parents and the students themselves. Set in policy, staff roles and responsibilities for *behaviour* management included:

- use of data to inform planning
- meeting and greeting students at the classroom door
- being inclusive and welcoming to all students
- differentiating
- cultivating positive relationships
- taking a restorative approach to behaviour management

Every student was allocated four achievement points linked to school values at the start of every lesson; all were perceived as aspiring, respectful, collaborative and resilient. Interestingly, teachers' use of achievement points was a trust factor raised by a number of research participants, one of whom, although routinely well behaved, reflected that inconsistent use of achievement points

> makes students feel left out, or like do they think I'm a bad kid or something. Or like you might as well stop trying to be good. It's hard work being good, it's easier to be bad than to be good.[63]

In the case study school, students could achieve additional points for a range of reasons, and there was a noticeable shift from the language of sanctions to the language of values, praise and achievement. Rather than selecting a fraction of behaviour from 'everything that could be known about a child', staff increasingly reached out non-judgementally to systemically vulnerable young people and listened to them, in a climate in which students were valued, supported and enabled to learn.[64] Sanctions remained available, but after-school and senior leadership detentions reduced significantly and no longer disproportionately reflected systemically vulnerable students. All staff received training on restorative conversations, and restorative sentence starters were printed on the reverse side of their school lanyards. Additionally, the attached educational psychologist's time included the delivery of attachment training in small staff groups over the course of a year, helping to build teachers' understanding and agency.

The case study school serves as just one example of what can be achieved through strategic leadership of inclusion. Although school and sociodemographic contexts differ, arguably broad-scale change is needed with collective commitments to policies that place inclusive, relational methods at the centre of teaching and learning.[65] When considering the disproportionate impact of fixed-term and permanent exclusions on systemically vulnerable students, 'relationality takes on profound significance'.[66] Moreover, experience points to a student cohort with complex psychological or developmental needs in many mainstream settings; thus, alongside inclusive systems, school-based inclusion centres enabling such students to access personalised timetables and additional specialist support would alleviate existing pressures on school staff. A recommendation for school funding to create internal inclusion centres was made to the department for education (DFE) in 2017,[67] and experience points to the inclusive benefits of flexible learning options for identified students in some subjects. Co-opting SENCos into senior leadership meetings is also a strong inclusive move; not only does it provide SENDCos with leadership insight and training from a whole school perspective, but it also provides a dedicated inclusive perspective for decision-makers. At the case study school, middle leaders were co-opted into senior leadership meetings as standard practice, and unsurprisingly the strength of middle leadership development was another factor highlighted by inspectors.

Concluding Thoughts

As identified, studies on a range of educational themes including governance, leadership, and culture point to the cultivation of relational trust among all stakeholders as an essential ingredient of sustainable educational reform.[68,69,70] Pertinent to the existing teacher recruitment and retention crisis, employees in an international business study reported that working in environments characterised by low levels of trust felt 'stressful, threatening, divisive, unproductive and tense'; conversely, working in high-trust work environments felt 'fun, supportive, motivating, productive and comfortable'.[71] Similarly, these contrasting feelings are undoubtedly reflected in the student experience too. If sustainable educational growth is a goal, measures to improve the holistic development of both students and staff are vital and an aspect often overlooked as a result of the persistent drive for academic excellence. The following abridged extract from a student's note to her teacher illustrates the value of holistic learning:

> You've been so supportive, whether that be through maths, school, or issues that I've had at home. While everyone as well as myself gave up on me, you remained positive which gave me hope and courage to try instead of giving up on everything. I hate maths, I hate it with

a passion but as well as teaching me maths you've also taught me not to give up on the challenges life throws at you. You've taught me more life skills than anyone ever has.[72]

This student failed her Maths GCSE, but she didn't give up, she attended college and passed an equivalent maths qualification. She trained and worked as a dental practitioner and some years later was accepted to study for a degree in psychology with a view to training as a therapist. Given her social, cultural and familial circumstances along with her behavioural track record, her onward journey could have been a different story. Fortunately, she benefited from an inclusive school infused with relational trust that genuinely aspired for every student, regardless of their systemic vulnerabilities.

Whilst operationalising relational trust is a research-based methodology for optimising inclusive practice which promotes collective learning, 'it takes immense courage and self-belief to stand up for what is right in today's culture'.[73] There will inevitably be opponents along the way, not least those who consider trust development to be a *soft* or *secondary* skill with imprecise outcomes. However, this is the opposite of the reality; overcoming the fear of vulnerability is a universally hard skill to master[74] and developing the courage to risk judgement or failure, arguably a mark of resilience and mental strength conducive to improved learning outcomes. To aid surety and metrics, student and department trust levels are measurable using trust surveys based on comparable representative samples of students and practitioners in the US[75]; undoubtedly, updated UK trust scales could also be developed. As evidenced, excellent practice already exists at school and individual levels, but new learnings need to be widely adopted to ensure an aligned system where trust and inclusivity provide value for all and practitioners share a collective will to collaborate rather than compete. As Margaret Heffernan's inspiring TED talk attests, if the only way the most individually productive, high-achieving people and organisations can be successful is by suppressing the productivity of the rest, 'we badly need to find a better way to work and a richer way to live'.[76]

Notes

1 Qvortrup A & Qvortrup L (2018). 'Inclusion: Dimensions of Inclusion in Education', *International Journal of Inclusive Education*, Vol. 22, No. 7, pp. 803–817, https://doi.org/10.1080/13603116.2017.1412506.
2 Qvortrup A & Qvortrup L (2018). 'Inclusion: Dimensions of Inclusion in Education', *International Journal of Inclusive Education*, Vol. 22, No. 7, pp. 803–817, https://doi.org/10.1080/13603116.2017.1412506.
3 Whitaker D (2021). 'The Kindness Principle', Independent Thinking Press.
4 Cabral-Gouveia C, Menezes I & Neves T (2023). 'Educational Strategies to Reduce the Achievement Gap: A Systematic Review, *Frontiers in Education*, Vol. 8, https://doi.org/10.3389/feduc.2023.1155741, pp. 1–15.

5 Children's Commissioner (2024). 'New Statistics Show a Huge Increase in the Number of Children Completely Missing Education', https://www.childrenscommissioner.gov.uk/blog/shocking-new-statistics-show-a-huge-increase-in-the-number-of-children-completely-missing-education/. Accessed 26.02.25.

6 Down B, Sullivan A, Tippett N, Johnson B, Manolev J & Robinson J (2024). 'What Is Missing in Policy Discourses about School Exclusions?', Taylor & Francis, https://www.tandfonline.com/doi/epdf/10.1080/17508487.2024.2312878?needAccess=true. Accessed 11.09.24.

7 DFE (2016) 'Educational Excellence Everywhere', https://assets.publishing.service.gov.uk/media/5a804face5274a2e8ab4f6b7/Educational_Excellence_Everywhere.pdf. Accessed 26.02.25.

8 HM Government (2022). 'Opportunity for All: Strong Schools with Great Teachers for Your Child', https://assets.publishing.service.gov.uk/media/62416cb5d3bf7f32add7819f/Opportunity_for_all_strong_schools_with_great_teachers_for_your_child__print_version_.pdf. Accessed 26.02.25.

9 Aynsley-Green A (2019). 'The British Betrayal of Childhood: Challenging Uncomfortable Truths and Bringing about Change', Routledge.

10 Aynsley-Green A (2019, p. 87). 'The British Betrayal of Childhood: Challenging Uncomfortable Truths and Bringing about Change', Routledge.

11 ISOS Partnership (2024). 'Towards an Effective and Financially Sustainable Approach to SEND in England', Independent Report commissioned by CCN (County Councils Network) and LGA (The Local Government Association), https://static1.squarespace.com/static/5ce55a5ad4c5c500016855ee/t/669fced acd1a1f608546f52b/1721749338168/SEND+report.pdf. Accessed 26.02.25.

12 ISOS Partnership (2024). 'Towards an Effective and Financially Sustainable Approach to SEND in England', Independent Report commissioned by CCN (County Councils Network) and LGA (The Local Government Association), https://static1.squarespace.com/static/5ce55a5ad4c5c500016855ee/t/669fced acd1a1f608546f52b/1721749338168/SEND+report.pdf. Accessed 26.02.25.

13 DFE & Department of Health (2014). SEND Code of Practice: 0–25 Years, https://www.gov.uk/government/publications/send-code-of-practice-0-to-25. Accessed 26.02.25.

14 Curren H, Moloney H, Heavy A & Boddison A (2018). 'It's about Time: The Impact of SENCO Workload on the Professional and the School', Bath Spa University, Nasen, National Education Union, https://neu.org.uk/latest/library/senco-workload-report. Accessed 10.09.24.

15 DFE (2024). 'Suspensions and Permanent Exclusions in England', https://explore-education-statistics.service.gov.uk/find-statistics/suspensions-and-permanent-exclusions-in-england. Accessed 26.02.25.

16 Shaw M & Audley J (2024). 'The Prevalence of School Exclusions in the UK, Their Root Causes, and the Importance of Preventative Offerings Over Reactive Interventions', Catch 22, https://www.catch-22.org.uk/resources/the-prevalence-of-school-exclusions-in-the-uk/. Accessed 10.09.24.

17 Cabral-Gouveia C, Menezes I & Neves T (2023). 'Educational Strategies to Reduce the Achievement Gap: A Systematic Review, *Frontiers in Education*, Vol. 8, https://doi.org/10.3389/feduc.2023.1155741, pp. 1–15.

18 Sahlberg P (2021). Finnish Lessons 3.0: What Can the World Learn from Educational Change in Finland?', Teachers College Press.

19 Aynsley-Green A (2019, p. 36). 'The British Betrayal of Childhood: Challenging Uncomfortable Truths and Bringing about Change', Routledge.

20 Nilholm C (2021). 'Research about Inclusive Education in 2020 – How Can We Improve Our Theories in Order to Change Practice?', *European Journal of Special Needs Education*, Vol. 26, No. 3, pp. 358–370.

21 Shaw M & Audley J (2024). 'The Prevalence of School Exclusions in the UK, Their Root Causes, and the Importance of Preventative Offerings Over Reactive Interventions', https://www.catch-22.org.uk/resources/the-prevalence-of-school-exclusions-in-the-uk/. Accessed 10.09.24.

22 Down B, Sullivan A, Tippett N, Johnson B, Manolev J & Robinson J (2024). 'What Is Missing in Policy Discourses about School Exclusions?', Taylor & Francis, https://www.tandfonline.com/doi/epdf/10.1080/17508487.2024.2312878?needAccess=true.

23 Cabral-Gouveia C, Menezes I & Neves T (2023). 'Educational Strategies to Reduce the Achievement Gap: A Systematic Review, *Frontiers in Education*, Vol. 8, https://doi.org/10.3389/feduc.2023.1155741, pp. 1–15.

24 Sharma U (2018). 'Preparing to Teach in Inclusive Classrooms', Oxford Research Encyclopaedias, Education, https://oxfordre.com/education/display/10.1093/acrefore/9780190264093.001.0001/acrefore-9780190264093-e-113. Accessed 20.09.24.

25 Sharma U (2018, p. 2). 'Preparing to Teach in Inclusive Classrooms', Oxford Research Encyclopaedias, Education, https://oxfordre.com/education/display/10.1093/acrefore/9780190264093.001.0001/acrefore-9780190264093-e-113. Accessed 20.09.24.

26 Cabral-Gouveia C, Menezes I & Neves T (2023). 'Educational Strategies to Reduce the Achievement Gap: A Systematic Review, *Frontiers in Education*, Vol. 8, https://doi.org/10.3389/feduc.2023.1155741, pp. 1–15.

27 O'Brien J (2016, p. 37). 'Don't Send Him in Tomorrow: Shining a Light on the Marginalised, Disenfranchised and Forgotten Children of Today's Schools', Independent Thinking Press.

28 Aynsley-Green A (2019). 'The British Betrayal of Childhood: Challenging Uncomfortable Truths and Bringing about Change', Routledge.

29 Curren H, Moloney H, Heavy A & Boddison A (2018, p. 2). 'It's about Time: The Impact of SENCO Workload on the Professional and the School', Bath Spa University, Nasen, National Education Union, https://neu.org.uk/latest/library/senco-workload-report. Accessed 10.09.24.

30 Curren H, Moloney H, Heavy A & Boddison A (2018). 'It's about Time: The Impact of SENCO Workload on the Professional and the School', Bath Spa University, Nasen, National Education Union, https://neu.org.uk/latest/library/senco-workload-report. Accessed 10.09.24.

31 Aynsley-Green A (2019). 'The British Betrayal of Childhood: Challenging Uncomfortable Truths and Bringing about Change', Routledge.

32 Ainscow M & Sandill A (2010, p. 407). 'Developing Inclusive Education Systems: The Role of Organisational Cultures and Leadership', *International Journal of Inclusive Education*, Vol. 14, No. 4, pp. 401–416.

33 Department of Education (2021, p. 11). 'Teachers' Standards: Guidance for School Leaders, School Staff and Governing Bodies', Ref: DEF-00066-2011, https://assets.publishing.service.gov.uk/media/61b73d6c8fa8f50384489c9a/Teachers__Standards_Dec_2021.pdf. Accessed 04.09.24.

34 Taylor SC (2017). 'Contested Knowledge: A Critical Review of the Concept of Differentiation in Teaching and Learning', *Warwick Journal of Education*, Vol. 1, pp. 55–68. https://journals.warwick.ac.uk/index.php/wjett/article/view/44. Accessed 26.02.25.

35 Taylor SC (2017). 'Contested Knowledge: A Critical Review of the Concept of Differentiation in Teaching and Learning', *Warwick Journal of Education*, Vol. 1, pp. 55–68. https://journals.warwick.ac.uk/index.php/wjett/article/view/44. Accessed 26.02.25.

36 Moore S (2016). 'One without the Other: Stories of Unity Through Diversity and Inclusion', Portage & Main Press.

37 Aynsley-Green A (2019, p. 127). 'The British Betrayal of Childhood: Challenging Uncomfortable Truths and Bringing about Change', Routledge.
38 Aynsley-Green A (2019). 'The British Betrayal of Childhood: Challenging Uncomfortable Truths and Bringing about Change', Routledge.
39 Messiou K (2019). 'Collaborative Action Research: Facilitating Inclusion in Schools', *Educational Action Research*, Vol. 27, No. 2, pp. 197–209.
40 Cabral-Gouveia C, Menezes I & Neves T (2023). 'Educational Strategies to Reduce the Achievement Gap: A Systematic Review, *Frontiers in Education*, Vol. 8, https://doi.org/10.3389/feduc.2023.1155741, pp. 1–15.
41 Sahlberg P (2021). Finnish Lessons 3.0: What Can the World Learn from Educational Change in Finland?', Teachers College Press.
42 Whitaker D (2021). 'The Kindness Principle', Independent Thinking Press.
43 Bennett T (2017, p. 8 & 9). 'Creating a Culture: How School Leaders Can Optimise Behaviour', Independent review of behaviour in schools, https://www.gov.uk/government/publications/behaviour-in-schools. Accessed 14.09.24.
44 Whitaker D (2021). 'The Kindness Principle', Independent Thinking Press.
45 Bennett T (2017, p. 41). 'Creating a Culture: How School Leaders Can Optimise Behaviour', Independent review of behaviour in schools, https://www.gov.uk/government/publications/behaviour-in-schools. Accessed 14.09.24.
46 Shaw M & Audley J (2024). 'The Prevalence of School Exclusions in the UK, Their Root Causes, and the Importance of Preventative Offerings Over Reactive Interventions', Catch 22, https://www.catch-22.org.uk/resources/the-prevalence-of-school-exclusions-in-the-uk/. Accessed 10.09.24.
47 Whitaker D (2021). 'The Kindness Principle', Independent Thinking Press.
48 Whitaker D (2021). 'The Kindness Principle', Independent Thinking Press.
49 Down B, Sullivan A, Tippett N, Johnson B, Manolev J & Robinson J (2024). 'What Is Missing in Policy Discourses about School Exclusions?', Taylor & Francis, https://www.tandfonline.com/doi/epdf/10.1080/17508487.2024.2312878?needAccess=true. Accessed 11.09.24.
50 Bishop S, Craven M, Galer D, Wilson T & Buggins-Clay P (2022). 'Literature Review-School Discipline', Intercultural Development Research Association, https://files.eric.ed.gov/fulltext/ED629271.pdf. Accessed 11.09.24.
51 Bishop S, Craven M, Galer D, Wilson T, & Buggins-Clay P (2022). 'Literature Review-School Discipline', Intercultural Development Research Association, https://files.eric.ed.gov/fulltext/ED629271.pdf. Accessed 11.09.24.
52 Senge PM (2006, p. 100). 'The Fifth Discipline: The Art & Practice of the Learning Organisation', Random House Business Books.
53 Down B, Sullivan A, Tippett N, Johnson B, Manolev J & Robinson J (2024). 'What Is Missing in Policy Discourses about School Exclusions?', Taylor & Francis, https://www.tandfonline.com/doi/epdf/10.1080/17508487.2024.2312878?needAccess=true.
54 Shaw M & Audley J (2024). 'The Prevalence of School Exclusions in the UK, Their Root Causes, and the Importance of Preventative Offerings Over Reactive Interventions', Catch 22, https://www.catch-22.org.uk/resources/the-prevalence-of-school-exclusions-in-the-uk/. Accessed 10.09.24.
55 Bishop S, Craven M, Galer D, Wilson T, & Buggins-Clay P (2022, p. 18). 'Literature Review-School Discipline', Intercultural Development Research Association, https://files.eric.ed.gov/fulltext/ED629271.pdf. Accessed 11.09.24.
56 Brown B (2018). 'Dare to Lead: Brave Work. Tough Conversations. Whole hearts', Penguin Random House.
57 Brown B (2018). 'Dare to Lead: Brave Work. Tough Conversations. Whole hearts', Penguin Random House.
58 Senge PM (2006, p. 100). 'The Fifth Discipline: The Art & Practice of the Learning Organisation', Random House Business Books.

59 Down B, Sullivan A, Tippett N, Johnson B, Manolev J & Robinson J (2024). 'What Is Missing in Policy Discourses about School Exclusions?', Taylor & Francis, https://www.tandfonline.com/doi/epdf/10.1080/17508487.2024.2312878? needAccess=true. Bishop S, Craven M, Galer D, Wilson T, & Buggins-Clay P (2022). 'Literature Review-School Discipline', Intercultural Development Research Association, https://files.eric.ed.gov/fulltext/ED629271.pdf. Accessed 11.09.24.

60 Cabral-Gouveia C, Menezes I & Neves T (2023). 'Educational Strategies to Reduce the Achievement Gap: A Systematic Review, *Frontiers in Education*, Vol. 8, https://doi.org/10.3389/feduc.2023.1155741, pp. 1–15.

61 Bishop S, Craven M, Galer D, Wilson T, & Buggins-Clay P (2022). 'Literature Review-School Discipline', Intercultural Development Research Association, https://files.eric.ed.gov/fulltext/ED629271.pdf. Accessed 11.09.24

62 Shaw M & Audley J (2024). 'The Prevalence of School Exclusions in the UK, Their Root Causes, and the Importance of Preventative Offerings Over Reactive Interventions', Catch 22, https://www.catch-22.org.uk/resources/the-prevalence-of-school-exclusions-in-the-uk/. Accessed 10.09.24.

63 Byrnell VH (2019, Appendix M, p. 1). Academic Paper, St Mary's University.

64 Aynsley-Green A (2019h, p. 50, citing Willow C). 'The British Betrayal of Childhood: Challenging Uncomfortable Truths and Bringing about Change', Routledge.

65 Down B, Sullivan A, Tippett N, Johnson B, Manolev J & Robinson J (2024). 'What Is Missing in Policy Discourses about School Exclusions?', Taylor & Francis, https://www.tandfonline.com/doi/epdf/10.1080/17508487.2024.2312878? needAccess=true.

66 Down B, Sullivan A, Tippett N, Johnson B, Manolev J & Robinson J (2024, p. 8). 'What Is Missing in Policy Discourses about School Exclusions?', Taylor & Francis, https://www.tandfonline.com/doi/epdf/10.1080/17508487.2024. 2312878?needAccess=true.

67 Bennett T (2017). 'Creating a Culture: How School Leaders Can Optimise Behaviour', Independent review of behaviour in schools, https://www.gov.uk/government/publications/behaviour-in-schools. Accessed 14.09.24.

68 Tschannen-Moran M (2017). 'Trust in Education', Oxford University Press, https://doi.org/10.1093/acrefore/9780190264093.013.79.

69 Sahlberg P (2021). 'Finnish Lessons 3.0: What Can the World Learn from Educational Change in Finland?', Teachers College Press.

70 Kaser L & Halbert J (2009, pp. 42–60). 'Trust-Relationships First', Leadership Mindsets: Innovation and Learning in the Transformation of Schools, Routledge.

71 Hurley RF (2006, npr). 'The Decision to Trust', Harvard Business Review, https://hbr.org/2006/09/the-decision-to-trust. Accessed 27.02.25.

72 Y11 Student (2017). Outer London state-maintained secondary school.

73 Aynsley-Green A (2019, p. 111). 'The British Betrayal of Childhood: Challenging Uncomfortable Truths and Bringing about Change', Routledge.

74 Brown B (2018). 'Dare to Lead: Brave Work. Tough Conversations. Whole hearts', Penguin Random House.

75 Adams CM (2013). 'Collective Trust: A Social Indicator of Instructional Capacity', *Journal of Educational Administration*, Vol. 51, No. 3, pp. 363–382, https://doi.org/10.1108/09578231311311519.

76 Heffernan M (2015). 'Forget the Pecking Order at Work', TEDWomen, https://www.ted.com/talks/margaret_heffernan_forget_the_pecking_order_at_work?subtitle=en. Accessed 08.10.24.

Epilogue

The Child in Front of Me

The child I was
Is the child in front of me
Searching for love and authenticity
I see loss and longing beneath innocent eyes
And sinews of shame taking root inside
The path may be rugged, stony and bare
Wounds inflicted, no self-care
Arrows of hurt darting around
A soul that's lost and waiting to be found
Like a horse in a desert dying of thirst
Exposed, defenceless, fearing the worst.

The child I was
Is the child in front of me
Searching for love and authenticity
The journey's long, there's a heart to explore
A heart with both open and bolted doors
But with each small step awareness grows
Of arenas of the soul that demand to be known.
The wait can be long at arena doors
The risk, hearts in pieces strewn over the floors
And the tempter's voice speaks soft and low
Shame is the thief that can steal the show
But it cannot survive the clear light of day
Connection's our friend and shame slinks away
Vulnerability exposed, we're learning anew
Courage is the way to a heart that's true.

The child I was
Is the child in front of me
Searching for love and authenticity
The road less travelled is the one assigned
Dancing with outliers of humankind
Meeting self and others with compassionate minds
Accepting the flaws within each of us we find
Close up to nature imperfection we'll see
Which is part of its beauty and majesty.
With fears unturned and minds growing strong
To ourselves and each other we know we belong.

The child in front of me
Is a calling and a plea
To trust and learn with a heart set free
And the scholarship of love is to serve in all we do
With a vulnerable, wild heart that's courageous and true.
Then children when in darkness, can smile with you and me
For it's only in the darkness that light is plain to see.

(Victoria Byrnell, 2021)

Appendix A

Suggested Strategies: Belonging

- Always put a smile on your face and make students feel welcome with a greeting every lesson, every day, especially those who experience a sense of difference or marginalised.
- Check the intonation in your voice is naturally warm/friendly – tell students if you are having a bad day and apologise if your manner seems unwelcoming.
- Be aware of your facial expression in repose! Check it out and practise smiling through your eyes.
- Pretend to like students you, personally, find *difficult to like* – there will always be some because we all have insecurities that can be triggered by students at a subconscious level.
- Ask students if they have had a good weekend, day, lesson, break/ lunch time as appropriate – show interest in them whether you are interested or not.
- Treat all students with the utmost courtesy and listen attentively to them *without starting to prepare a response in your mind*, regardless of your preconceptions or possible misconceptions. This is more difficult than we think because most people listen with the intent to reply rather than understand.
- Talk to students about seating positions – some students have genuine reasons for wanting to sit away from or with particular students, so be curious; seek to find out more and be accommodating.
- *Never* take student attempts to reject you or their work personally, they are simply seeking to avoid painful feelings which we may not understand or connect with.
- Find reasons and ways to appreciate students for who they are, their differences and their struggles and model love and acceptance towards unpopular or uncool students whilst maintaining boundaries. This is powerful practice.

Appendix B

Suggested Strategies: Learning Lessons

Vulnerability

- Be comfortable talking about feelings in lessons – they are a universal language. For example, as a greeting 'How are we all feeling today? Give some examples – happy, anxious, sad, etc. Or 'I'm feeling a bit ... today because ...' Create feelings boards with students to use in tutor sessions to stimulate their emotional language and self-awareness.
- *Listen* with as much passion as you talk – aim for a 70% listening – 30% talking ratio. We connect emotionally when we listen intently, thoughtfully and silently. Listening helps us recognise vulnerable emotions which underlie behaviours.
- Use emotionally literate language and quietly give a name to the way a distressed student may be feeling. For example, 'I notice you seem angry, I notice you seem sad, I notice you seem worried'. This will provide instant reassurance and provides *emotional holding* for the student.[1] Students are invariably quick to correct mistaken perceptions and communicate what they are actually feeling when we get it wrong.
- Be attuned to times when you feel *at risk, uncertain and emotionally exposed*. Practise identifying the underlying emotion and accepting the discomfort. Emotions do not come to stay they come to pass. Give yourself and your students permission to feel vulnerable – it's human, normal and necessary.
- To learn more about vulnerability, take 20 minutes to watch 'The Power of Vulnerability'[2] which is among the five most-viewed TED talks in the world. Alternative read Professor Brene Brown's books on vulnerability and leadership.

Learning Strategies

- Ensure all starter activities are mastery tasks, i.e. everyone can achieve them. Pay attention to your least able students and those who consistently find it difficult to settle. Repeat the favourites as often as you like. Predictability and routine work well at the start of every lesson.

- Speak simply and clearly, intentionally reduce the pace of your talk and ask for a volunteer to explain the task you have set. If s/he has difficulty explaining, repeat – clearer and simpler. This will facilitate understanding for students with a range of language difficulties.
- Impress on students that teachers are responsible for explaining things in a way they can understand, just as they are responsible for ensuring work is accessible for all students. Encourage a classroom climate in which speaking up is positively encouraged.
- Ensure students have access to written instructions or be prepared to repeat them as many times as necessary. Never assume students have not listened well – we do not know all the factors affecting their attention spans and difficulties with attention and working memory are extremely frustrating for students too.
- Vulnerability and learning happen in the space between teachers and students so reduce teacher talk to give students the time and space they need to learn. Try recording a normal lesson and note the time you spend talking in relation to the time students spend learning.
- Reassure students repeatedly that mistakes are key to the process of learning and they are allowed to get things wrong. Tell them how you feel when you make mistakes and give examples of mistakes that have helped you learn.
- Tell students there are no stupid ideas or answers – it is a measure and mark of their courage that they are prepared to have a go and engage in the vulnerable process of learning. If student questions seem irrelevant, always demonstrate a curious approach – they may lack the language to ask the questions they need answers to.
- Present new material in small, achievable steps. The chunking technique is a recommended strategy which helps all students to learn well, particularly those with language and processing difficulties.
- Provide scaffolding for students who refuse to work. Some students think 'If I don't try, I can't fail'. Be supportive, write the title, start the work, and see if they can risk just a little bit. Ask if they would like a peer to support them. If not, arrange to complete the work when you are able to give them individual support.
- Speak privately with students who consistently refuse to work to find out more about the problem. The message is, 'I will keep teaching you because I believe in you and I want you to achieve'. Tell me how I can support you better to … Would it help if I …?
- It is often helpful to give students a choice of task based on whether they are *feeling confident, need practice* or *are not quite there yet.* Developing the discipline of preparing lessons in this way becomes habitual and benefits all students.

- Present power points on cream backgrounds with a cursive, dark font and keep them as uncluttered as possible. Highlight or colour code key words or tasks. Provide an agenda for the lesson which students can refer to. This will benefit a range of student needs.
- Ask students to help you by scoring every lesson out of 10 for how well they think they have learnt in the lesson. It takes only seconds to write this down and is a helpful tool for reflection and reflexivity, both yours and theirs. Experience suggests students are generally very honest when asked to score their learning.

Cultivating Trustworthiness

- **Accountability:** *Apologise to students* when you get it wrong and make amends. We all make mistakes, and saying sorry can feel vulnerable, especially if we've made a poor judgement call or feel our reputation is at stake. The benefits of apologising to students cannot be overstated in respect of building trust:

   Teachers need to say sorry more to gain trust from students, so they can come to them when they need help or anything.[3]

   It's important to realise when people are hurt and teachers have to realise when they've gone too far and say sorry. Teachers saying sorry makes the teacher and the student feel better.[4]

   Distinguish the accountability of trust from performance-related accountability which is counter-productive to promoting reciprocal vulnerability practice if it entails judgement. When undergoing educational reform in the 1990s, it is noteworthy that Finland chose professional trust as an overarching aim, in contrast to the UK's aim of accountability.
- **Reliability:** *Carry out actions that you say you will.* At work, this necessitates staying aware of your strengths and weaknesses and not overpromising.[5] For participants, professional reliability was straightforward – it meant teachers *turning up, explaining clearly, ensuring work and homework are doable and keeping order.*
- **Integrity:** *Practice your values* rather than simply professing them, displaying them or referring to school mission statements. Sometimes rather than acting in a way that is value-driven, we choose the easy option or avoid acting altogether. However, practising values is essential to operationalising trust. Focus on *two key values* and *use them to guide your daily behaviours* towards others. For example, if a value you choose is trust, practise trust-building strategies.

- **Support:** *Ask for the support you need* and be willing to *give uncon-ditional support to others.* Help and support are important aspects of trustworthiness (see Appendix I).
- **Emotional Safety:** Consistently practise *care, connection and empa-thy* and trust students by *giving them the benefit of the doubt.* There is often more to situations than meets the eye, and it is advantageous to remain neutral and follow up later, rather than to blame or accuse carelessly, especially in front of peers (see Appendix E).
- **Non-judgement:** Refrain from making *moralistic* judgements about students; choose to believe they are *doing the best they can* and seek to understand the emotions underlying their behaviours. It is easy to assume people can do better, but this is more complex than we might think, raising questions about barriers to change and support needs (see Appendix G).
- **Boundaries:** Boundary setting is important to well-being and ensures that clear messages are communicated about behaviours that are out-side an individual's or organisational values.

  For example: 'I need you to respect this boundary (be explicit) because (state value/principle) is important. If you're unclear about what's okay or not okay, please ask'.
- **The Vault:** A safe container for other people's experiences or for in-formation others choose to share.[6] The Vault protects people from breaches of confidentiality as well as idle gossip and is demonstrated by:

  - Keeping confidences
  - Not sharing information which is not the recipients to share

Notes

1 Greenhalgh P (1994). 'Emotional Growth and Learning', Routledge.
2 Brown B (2010). 'The Power of Vulnerability', TEDxHouston, https://www.youtube.com/watch?v=iCvmsMzlF7o. Accessed 24.02.25.
3 Byrnell VH (2019, Appendix M, p. 5). Academic Paper, St Mary's University.
4 Byrnell VH (2019, Appendix M, p. 5). Academic Paper, St Mary's University.
5 Brown B (2018b). Academic Paper, St Mary's University.
6 Brown B (2015, p. 199). 'Rising Strong: If We Are Brave Enough, Often Enough, We Will Fall', Vermillion, Penguin Random House UK.

Appendix C

Suggested Strategies: Empathy and Inclusive Behaviour Management

- Learn the empathy attributes and practice them: (i) take the perspective of others, (ii) stay out of judgement, (iii) connect with others' emotions and (iv) communicate understanding of others' emotions. Pay attention to whether you are connecting emotionally with others feelings or expressing sympathy or reassurance. Avoid over-sharing personal experiences, downplaying the situation or giving advice.
- Practise self-compassion and monitor your self-talk carefully. If you notice you are berating yourself, try and reframe your inner conversation. Realise you did the best you could at the time and use the experience for learning.
- Praise *desired* student behaviours *first*. It is easy to be distracted by unwanted behaviours but praise first sends a powerful message of connection to students.
- Use eye contact and non-verbal gestures wherever possible to support behaviour requests. For example, flat hand being lowered (sit down), hand to ear (listening), finger to mouth (quiet please), revolving finger (turn around), hand to head (think), show five digits, mime *take 5*, then point to door (take time out).
- Avoid using negative or confrontational language. Clearly and simply state the desired behaviour, ending with a thank you. This communicates that you anticipate cooperation and expect the best. For example, 'Aaron, sitting quietly in your seat now, thank you. Sophie, paying attention and listening now, thank you. Theo, break time's over, back to work mode now, thank you'.
- Try using (although not overusing) the phrase 'I'm choosing to ignore ...' to avoid confrontation. Emotionally aroused students are often looking for an outlet, so don't give them one. For example, 'I'm choosing to ignore your rudeness' sends a clear, public message that the student has overstepped a boundary, *but you will address it when you are ready to do so*. Continue the lesson. If the behaviour

continues, you could try it once more, for example, 'I'm still choosing to ignore your rudeness, have you made a start yet?' If they put it right great, if not set an activity and *quietly* speak to the student. Use emotionally literate language. 'I notice you seem angry, but the rudeness is unacceptable. Do you need support, is everything OK?' If the student remains unresponsive and unable to learn in class, they may need time out. This is not failure; it is noticing, connection, upholding boundaries, support and trust building. You can follow up at a suitable time.

- *Give take up time* and *walk away* if a student point blank refuses to respond to a request. It is one of the most challenging behaviours to be confronted with and triggers huge vulnerability in teachers, but remember, the student is emotionally stuck. It is not a challenge to your personal authority, and if appropriate, *you can decide to change your mind.* For example, 'Actually I think it's best you stay there Sarah, Lauren would you mind moving instead?' Or 'Perhaps you need some thinking time? I'll come back to you in a few minutes'. These types of responses are good examples of teachers modelling vulnerability well. The outcome is uncertain – notice and accept the vulnerability.

- Find opportunities to tell students that they are kind/considerate/polite, they are hardworking/talented/funny, they make you feel proud/happy. Whether you believe it or not, their self-perceptions will begin to change. A colleague of mine recounted how she would tell a challenging student, Zara, in her tutor group that she was 'the sunshine in her life'. When she subsequently told another sad, systemically vulnerable student that he was her favourite, he replied that he knew he wasn't because Zara was her sunshine. She replied 'And you are the moonlight'. The student beamed.

- Praise all positive social interaction that you observe. Be explicit, for example, 'You are listening really well to Jordan's point of view', 'that's kind of you to let Kamil go first', 'you are a good friend to support Cameron'.

- Praise students for the courage to be honest, but don't expect truth, loyalty or respect as a matter of course. These attributes are only likely to be demonstrated by students who feel secure and loved. Students live out their experiences, and honesty, loyalty and respect may only be gained when trust is established.

- If sanctions are necessary, communicate *quietly and privately* with the student. Avoid making sanctions public, and if the student him/herself chooses to do so in an attempt to gain attention, you can simply walk away and say 'end of conversation'.

- Give students responsibilities, ask for their help, and allow them access to trips and positive experiences. Be wary of linking responsibilities and positive experiences to rewards; the benefits to self-esteem and trust building are invaluable.

Appendix D

Suggested Strategies: Shame Talk

- *Learn* the defensive responses to shame and look out for students who regularly use shame shields in your lessons. (i) Moving Against, (ii) Moving Away and (iii) Moving Toward. This will be the first step to understanding more about their shame triggers.
- Start a conversation with colleagues or your department about shame and its impact on student behaviours and learning. Collaboratively identify students who regularly use shame shields to increase awareness and consistency of practitioner responses.
- *Practise* the empathy attributes outlined in Chapter 3 – students will not judge you for getting it wrong, and you will begin to identify empathy hits and misses by their responses. The aim is to connect with their feelings to alleviate feelings of isolation. Encourage them to be kind to themselves.
- Recognise and accept that developing trust with highly shame-prone students will take time and support. Sometimes, it will require referral to therapeutic specialists if shame is embedded from adverse childhood experiences. Experience suggests one of the greatest casualties of the austerity years is a reduction in well-being and counselling services in schools. However, we must continue to press for appropriate provision where it is most needed.
- If you suspect students are immobilised by shame, aim to give them time, space and kindness.
- If you experience a student using the 'Moving Against' shield and empathetic approaches fail, the student will invariably need time out in a safe space. Shame-induced anger is an intense fear response – the fear of disconnection or possibly a relived shame experience from the past. In this state, students are compromised in their ability to self-regulate and recognising this is helpful for you and the student. Remaining calm, decisive and confident at such times will provide safety for you and others.

- Recommended reading: Brene Brown (2012) '*Daring Greatly: How the Courage to be Vulnerable Transforms the Way We Live, Love, Parent and Lead*', Chapter 3, Understanding and Combating Shame, Penguin Random House UK.

Appendix E

Suggested Strategies: Emotional Safety and Self-Protection

- Be alert to the self-protection mechanisms students may be using to avoid feeling vulnerable, especially when learning. Remain curious, empathise and offer support.
- Model emotional regulation and be consistent in your responses. If you feel angry, walk away and breathe. Shouting and careless use of sanctions will undermine trust. If you are drawn into an argument, try telling students you are *choosing to let them have the last word*. Remember the eyes and ears of all students are on you.
- If students are angry, give them time and space. Talk exacerbates emotional arousal and challenge, especially for students who struggle with language. If students are acting out, give directed time out as discreetly as possible, preferably accompanied, even by a responsible peer. On average, it takes an angry student half an hour before their rational brain starts functioning.
- Avoidance is a common response to feeling afraid or worried and is an armoured behaviour. Always take the presentation of fear or anxiety seriously; never downplay it or assume students are making up excuses simply to avoid doing something.
- Always address students behaviours which fall outside organisational values, either witnessed or reported by students. Sometimes, it may seem easier to avoid acting, but student safety is a priority, and every member of the community shares the responsibility to uphold values. State the boundaries clearly and calmly using a status master approach.
- Remember to greet students at the classroom door which promotes students' emotional safety and readiness for learning.
- Never dismiss an idea or say it's wrong. Instead ask 'Why do you think that?' or 'Nearly there'.[1]

- Be *relatable* and make time to get to know your students. Students will be more confident to get things wrong when they believe you will try and help them to get things right 'just like a family would'.[2]

Notes

1 Byrnell VH (2019, Appendix M, p. 3). 'Academic Paper and Conference Presentation', St Mary's University.
2 Byrnell VH (2019, Appendix M, p. 3). 'Academic Paper and Conference Presentation', St Mary's University.

Appendix F

Suggested Strategies: Imagine the Possibilities

- Aim to have fun with students in lessons. This starts by greeting students with a smile and adopting a positive, encouraging attitude towards all students.
- Try introducing lessons with play-based approaches to learning at key times of the day when students can struggle to remain focused. There are play-based approaches which facilitate skill-building in every subject – for example, strategy, literacy, maths and science games as well as creative challenges. Experience suggests there is a great deal to be learned about students from their play and they engage and work harder when you need them to, as a consequence.
- Log onto the SOLE website https://startsole.org/, and if possible, timetable some information and communication technology (ICT)-based lessons where your students can engage in self-orientated learning, focusing on big questions relevant to your subject.
- Consider showing students funny video clips for light relief or teach students a subject-related song. It is heartwarming to hear classes of secondary students singing enthusiastically in their language lessons and invariably their teachers are also smiling. Singing does not need to be limited to language lessons; students enjoy maths rap too.
- Refrain from depriving systemically vulnerable students of break times unless there is a recognised risk to safety; typically, the students most in need of the benefits of play are those who miss out the most, both in home and school environments.

Appendix G

Suggested Strategies: Non-Judgement Is Wise Judgement

- Practise empathy, curiosity and educationally wise judgement: 'I notice you're struggling to do as asked, tell me more, tell me how this is for you'?
- Notice the judgement habits you practice with students and monitor your language carefully. Behaviours may fall outside organisational values, but students need to feel valued regardless. Remember that *good hearts sometimes choose poor methods.*
- When student behaviours are ethically questionable, begin conversations along the lines 'I know you have a good heart and this behaviour (be explicit) is not aligned with your values, can you tell me what's going on?'
- Consider displaying the following poem in your classroom and staffroom to promote the trustworthy characteristic of non-judgement. If shame is present, there is always a risk of unhealthy moralistic judgement by adults and students alike.

Judge Softly

Pray, don't find fault with the child who limps
Or stumbles along the road,
Unless you have worn the shoes she wears
Or struggled beneath her load.

There may be tacks in her shoes that hurt
Though hidden away from view,
Or the burden she bears, placed on your back
Might cause you to stumble too.

Don't smear the child who's down today
Unless you have felt the blow

That caused her fall, or felt the shame
That only the fallen know.

You may be strong, but still the blows
That were hers, if dealt to you
In the self-same way, at the self-same time
Might cause you to stagger too.

Don't be too harsh with the child who sins
Or pelt her with words or stones
Unless you are sure – yes, double sure
That you have no sins of your own.

For you know, perhaps, if the tempter's voice
Should whisper as soft to you
As it did to her when she went astray,
'Twould cause you to falter, too.

Try walking a mile in the child's shoes,
Don't criticise, blame or accuse.
And find a way to take the time
To reflect on your own views.

I believe you'd be surprised to see
You've been narrow-minded, even blind.
For there're children from all walks of life
With too much worry on their minds.

We'll be known forever by the tracks we leave
In other people's lives.
So open your heart, put on her shoes
And see through the child's eyes.

>   (Source: Version of original poem by
>   Lathrap M T (1895) 'Judge Softly')

Appendix H

Suggested Strategies: Gratitude Gateways

- Create an ethos of gratitude in your school by remembering to thank colleagues and staff repeatedly, from management to caretakers and cleaning staff. In emails and all communications, try to communicate at least one positive message.
- Find as many reasons as you can to thank students for what they do and say. Thank them for their time, contributions, good behaviours, politeness, patience, turning up, being on time, etcetera.
- Introduce gratitude practice with students. For example, in tutor time or personal, social and health education lessons, introduce a daily/weekly gratitude session – a sharing event, or a note/letter writing exercise to express appreciation for someone or something in their lives.
- Visually expose students to the situations of other young people in the world who live in life-limiting or dangerous circumstances, not with the intention of making comparisons, but because studies suggest that contemplating endings makes people more grateful for the life they currently have. There is a caveat, as always, for the need for sensitivity towards students who have personal experiences of grief or loss.
- Model the ability to savour positive experiences with students – thank them for their contribution to making lessons memorable or enjoyable.
- Demonstrate impeccable manners and speak to students as you would speak to a respected colleague or a friend to reinforce respect and appreciation for others.
- Develop the habit of thinking of something to be grateful for each day. For example, if you wake up feeling tired or out of sorts, 'think of what a precious privilege it is to be alive, to breathe, to think, to enjoy, to love'.[1]

Note

1 Aurelius M (161–180 AD). 'Meditations', Penguin Classics.

Appendix I

Suggested Strategies: Support Matters

- Discuss as a class how students find it easiest to ask for help and display the ideas they come up with. Systemically vulnerable students are likely to continue to find asking for help challenging, so check in with them as often as you can and be ready to offer support.
- Share with students the things you find difficult and need help with. Ask students for their support whenever an opportunity arises.

  'When I've needed help she'll help me or if she needs help, I'll help her.'[1]

- Use students' natural inclination to be helpful as a strategy; helping can boost their self-esteem by giving them a sense of purpose and value.

Suggested Strategies for Neurologically Diverse Students

- Building positive relationships is key to working successfully with attention-deficit hyperactivity disorder (ADHD) students; find out their interests and the people who are important to them, communicate genuine warmth and take opportunities to praise seemingly routine behaviours such as settling, shifting attention or ignoring distractions.
- When a relationship is built, be explicit in the way you connect with students. For example, 'I need you shift your attention now, I know this is what you find difficult, what support do you need to focus on the next task?' Or 'I notice you seem very tired today; I understand how that feels, try and relax and do the best you can'.
- ADHD and its associated anxiety can often be passed on genetically. Make specific efforts to build positive relationships with parents and carers and communicate positive feedback. This can help to reduce school-related anxieties in the home environment which are invariably passed on to students.

- Seat purposefully *in collaboration with* the student. Contrary to what teachers often insist on, some ADHD students are far more comfortable sitting at the back of classrooms where their anxiety levels are reduced.
- Be mindful that seemingly innocent peers know only too well how to distract and raise anxiety levels in ADHD students.
- Aim to stand close to ADHD students when speaking, whether at the front or back of the classroom. When necessary, attract the student's attention by using their name calmly and making eye contact. Be aware that students with comorbid autism may be unable to reciprocate eye contact.
- Allow fiddle objects, doodling or drawing, but remain calm and patient when directing students to start work – remember *shifting attention is their struggle* and this is when support is most needed.
- Give one instruction at a time and chunk tasks into achievable steps. Provide scaffolding and support to begin writing tasks (dysgraphia and processing difficulties affect 50% of ADHD students). The chunking strategy is recommended for all students affected by language or working memory difficulties and compromises none.
- Intervene early, at the first signs of impulsive, restless or distracting behaviours. You could try:

  - Giving a classroom responsibility.
  - Asking the student to run an errand for you – sometimes a prepared envelope to take to reception can work well if reception staff are briefed and willing.
  - ADHD students also frequently lose water bottles and get overheated, so allow them to get a drink of water.

- If school arrangements allow and symptoms are severe (sometimes symptoms can vary according to the time of day), offer the option of working in a support room, presented as a positive choice. Students with ADHD often benefit from working in support rooms with access to lesson power points on laptops, as evidenced during the COVID pandemic. Be willing to listen to their suggestions about alternative ways to access learning successfully and permit rest breaks if practicable.
- If students become argumentative or aggressive do not get drawn in – remember shame is a hallmark of ADHD. Use a strategy that works to give students time out to calm down whilst preserving their dignity. If possible, agree a strategy collaboratively with the student in private.
- Sanctions may be necessary, but be realistic about their efficacy in changing behaviours. Building relationships will *always* be more

successful and taking the time to meet with ADHD students 1:1 to discuss the best way to support them can produce unexpectedly positive results.

- See ADHD students as individuals with values and character traits that define them more than their neurological traits do. Few ADHD students will leave school without a battering to their self-esteem and some degree of social rejection.[2]

Notes

1 Byrnell VH (2019, Appendix M, p. 1). 'Academic Paper and Conference Presentation', St Mary's University.
2 Mahony E (2019). 'Better Late Than Never: Understand, Survive and Thrive Midlife ADHD Diagnosis', Trigger.

Appendix J

Outline Policy Proposal

POLICY TITLE	RELATIONAL TRUST DEVELOPMENT
PURPOSE	To operationalise the principles and components of relational trust in schools
SUMMARY	Rationale, objectives and responsibilities to support trust development policy implementation
RELATED POLICIES	Code of Conduct; Equality Objectives; SEND; Anti-bullying; Curriculum principles

Rationale

Research points to relational trust as pivotal to empowering all members of school communities to participate, collaborate and maximise educational outcomes for all students. Relational trust necessitates reframing traditional understandings of human vulnerability as weakness, and developing the courage to be vulnerable through which relational trust, learning and resilience arise. A range of factors pertinent to schools including the vulnerable nature of learning, organisational hierarchy and systemically vulnerable student populations increase the need to guard against self-protective routines, relational breakdown and distrust. The components of trust can be learned and operationalised so that relational trust permeates school cultures, promoting inclusive school communities which enable staff and students to thrive.

Definitions:

Vulnerability: 'the seat of human emotion experienced at times of 'uncertainty, risk, and emotional exposure'.[1]

Trust: 'the willingness to be vulnerable and risk making something you value vulnerable to another person's actions'.[2]

Distrust: 'what is important to me is not safe with this person in this situation (or any situation).[3]

Objectives:

- To provide professional development opportunities for practitioners to:
  - Develop a shared understanding of vulnerability and the components of relational trust
  - Understand the links between teacher-student trust and learning
  - Understand the links between vulnerability and empowerment
  - Recognise a range of defence mechanisms typically used as a barrier to vulnerability which impact negatively on relationships
  - Explore the concept of shame and its impacts
- To collectively create a school Trust Development Charter outlining practice which aligns with and underpins core school values
- To improve teacher-student interactions and behaviour for learning
- To increase student engagement and learning outcomes
- To develop emotional learning and trust within the student community

Responsibilities

Headteacher

- Organise introduction of relational trust development initiative through whole school INSET
- Establish a cross-curricula trust development team and invite interested practitioners to join
- Commit time and capacity to enable whole staff training and engagement
- Promote the policy aims in the school and wider community
- Develop a non-judgemental performance management system aligned with the accountability component of relational trust and establish a protocol for productive feedback
- Promote emotional literacy development time for students within existing curriculum time, for example, in collaboration with tutors and/or PSHE teachers.

Trust Development Team

- Conduct staff and student trust surveys to establish baseline trust levels

- Plan and deliver collaborative CDP sessions aligned with policy objectives

  - Develop shared understanding of vulnerability and relational trust
  - Discuss and learn about specific components of relational trust and its barriers
  - Operationalise core values by collaboratively compiling behaviour exemplars
  - Model and promote shared language and relational trust behaviours
  - Explore restorative conversations based on relational trust practice

- Devise a realistic timetable for implementation
- Agree performance indicators for monitoring and evaluation
- Ensure all staff have access to training and CPD materials
- Monitor, evaluate and provide regular feedback to school leadership team

Whole Staff

- To commit to continuous personal and professional development on relational trust
- To operationalise relational trust through interactions and practice
- To use shared language that embodies best practice
- To support processes to operationalise relational trust development in the school
- To work collaboratively and empathetically to resolve barriers
- To engage students in developing their emotional literacy skills

Notes

1 Brown B (2018, p. 19). 'Dare to Lead: Brave Work. Tough Conversations. Whole Hearts', Penguin Random House UK.
2 Feltman C (2009a, p. 9). 'The Thin Book of Trust: An Essential Primer for Building Trust at Work', Thin Book Publishing Co.
3 Feltman C (2009b, p. 8). 'The Thin Book of Trust: An Essential Primer for Building Trust at Work', Thin Book Publishing.

Appendix K

SEND Code of Practice (2014)

Categories of Need

- *Cognition and Learning (C&L)*
  Moderate Learning Difficulties (MLD)
  Specific Learning Difficulties (SpLD), e.g. dyslexia, dyscalculia, dysgraphia
- *Communication and Interaction (C&I)*
  Speech, Language and Communication Needs (SLCN)
  Autism Spectrum Disorder (ASD)
- *Social, Emotional and Mental health (SEMH)*
  Attention-Deficit Hyperactivity Disorder (ADHD)
  Oppositional Defiance Disorder (ODD)
  Attachment Disorders
  Eating Disorders
  Anxiety Disorders
- *Physical Difficulties (PD)*
  Hearing Impaired (HI)
  Vision Impaired (VI)
  Cerebral Palsy
  Dyspraxia
  Other identified physical needs

Co-morbidity

Two or more concurrent areas of need, often referred to as complex needs. Some commonly found comorbidities are:

e.g. ADHD and dyslexia
ADHD and dysgraphia

ADHD and autism
Autism and Speech and Language
Cognition and Learning and Speech and Language

The needs listed in each category are those most commonly identified.

Appendix L

Screening Tests

Cognitive Ability Tests Explained

Cognitive ability tests provide an idea of cognitive ability and are an indicative tool alongside a number of other formal and teacher assessments which can be used to build a picture of students' strengths and weaknesses. It is important to ensure all students have access to information and communication technology (ICT) and equipment in good working order.

Quantitative Reasoning: Assesses numerical problem-solving skills, covering areas such as basic arithmetic, logical reasoning and mathematical analysis.

Spatial Reasoning: Assesses students' capability to visualize and manipulate shapes in their mind's eye.

Non-Verbal Reasoning: Assesses students' abilities to identify patterns, solve spatial problems and deduce logical relationships without relying on language.

Verbal Reasoning: Assesses skills in understanding and manipulating language, encompassing vocabulary, comprehension and verbal analogies.

Average Range: 85–111
Gifted Range: 120 or higher
Below Average: 85 or lower

Suggested Indicators

- Comparatively lower scores in *quantitative* or *verbal* reasoning can point to specific learning difficulties consistent with dyslexic or dyscalculic characteristics.

- A marked difference between *verbal* and *non-verbal* reasoning scores can point to dyslexic characteristics in students of any ability level, including gifted students who may benefit from using ICT as a normal method of working for extended writing tasks.
- Below average CAT scores can be indicative of learning difficulties for students who teachers need to check in with more regularly in class.
- *Non-verbal* reasoning is a useful assessment for students with English as a foreign language as there is no reading or English language knowledge required.
- As a 'rule of thumb', students with below average mean scores should be known to Learning Support Departments.

The Digit Memory Test

An extremely useful test to identify students with working memory difficulties and/or processing difficulties (where the gap between scores for digits forwards and backwards is greater than three). Age range: 6-Adult

Downloadable, printable resources and instructions provided on the link below.

Top tip: practice using it with a colleague, partner or child before use.

https://getintoneurodiversity.com/wp-content/uploads/2021/05/Digit-Memory-Test.pdf

ADHD Checklists

The checklists below are compiled from the Diagnostic and Statistical Manual of Mental Disorders. They are useful to identify characteristics of three presentations of attention-deficit hyperactivity disorder (ADHD):

i Inattentive.
ii Hyperactive and Impulsive.
iii Combined Presentation.

- Students presenting with inattentive characteristics of ADHD can often be overlooked and may persistently underachieve.

Experience points to discussions with parents being particularly useful when students assess themselves as meeting the criteria on the Student Checklist. Some parents will be struggling with behaviours at home and raising awareness is a starting point for further investigation and understanding.

ADHD Checklist (Student Perspective)

Inattentive Presentation

Trait	Almost Never	Some-times	Often	Very Often
I struggle to give close attention to details and make careless mistakes in schoolwork or with other activities				
I have trouble holding my attention on tasks or play activities				
People seem to think I'm not listening when they speak to me directly				
I lose focus and become side-tracked when given instructions or finished schoolwork or chores				
I have trouble organising tasks and activities				
I avoid, dislike or am reluctant to do tasks that require mental effort over a long period of time (such as school or homework)				
I lose things I need for tasks and activities (e.g. pencils, books, wallets, keys, mobile phones)				
I am easily distracted				
I am forgetful in daily activities				
TOTAL SCORES				

Six or more symptoms (Often or Very Often) for children up to age 16, or 5 or more for adolescents aged seventeen and adults.

Hyperactive and Impulsive Presentation

Trait	Almost Never	Some-times	Often	Very Often
I notice that I fidget or tap hands or feet, or squirm in my seat				
I leave my seat in situations when remaining in my seat is expected				
I run about or climb in situations where it is not appropriate OR I notice that I feel restless				
I am 'on the go', acting as if 'driven by a motor'				
I talk excessively				
I blurt out answers before a question has been completed				
I notice that I interrupt or intrude on others (e.g. butt into conversations or games)				
TOTAL SCORES				

Combined presentation is 6 or more symptoms of both presentations from each list (Often or Very Often) for children up to age 16, and 5 of each for adolescents and adults.

ADHD Checklist (Teacher or Parent Perspective of Student)

Inattentive Presentation

Trait	Almost Never	Some-times	Often	Very Often
Fails to give close attention to details and make careless mistakes in schoolwork or with other activities				
Has trouble holding attention on tasks or play activities				
Does not seem to listen when spoken to directly				
Does not follow through on instructions and fails to finish schoolwork (e.g. loses focus, becomes side-tracked)				
Has trouble organising tasks and activities				
Avoids, dislikes or is reluctant to do tasks that require mental effort over a long period of time (such as school or homework)				
Loses things necessary for tasks and activities (e.g. pencils, books, wallets, paperwork, eyeglasses, mobile phones)				
Is easily distracted				
Is forgetful in daily activities				
TOTAL SCORES				

Six or more symptoms (Often or Very Often) for children up to age 16 or 5 or more for adolescents aged 17 and adults.

Hyperactive and Impulsive Presentation

Trait	Almost Never	Some-times	Often	Very Often
Fidgets with or tap hands or feet, or squirms in seat				
Leaves seat in situations when remaining in my seat is expected				
Runs about or climbs in situations where it is not appropriate OR for adolescents/adults, seems restless				
'On the go', acting as if 'driven by a motor'				
Talks excessively				
Blurts out answers before a question has been completed				
Interrupts or intrudes on others (e.g. butt into conversations or games)				
TOTAL SCORES				

Combined presentation is 6 or more symptoms of both presentations from each list (Often or Very Often) for children up to age 16, and 5 of each for adolescents and adults.

Emotional Literacy

Assessment and Intervention photocopiable resources available for Primary and Secondary age students. Can be administered manually or using ICT (disk included).

Multi-user, indefinite license at an affordable price (secondhand copies are also available from various sellers). Profits go towards SEND (special educational needs and disabilities) charities as specified by the Southampton Psychology Service which compiled the assessments and resources.

Top tip: read the accompanying information and scoring systems carefully. There can be an anomaly in a student's result if they lack self-awareness and score themselves as well-above average in direct contrast to well-below average perceptions of their teacher and/or parent. Following intervention, the student's perception can change to well-below average which demonstrates progress has been made.

Cheapest seller found: Teaching Times Bookshop

https://www.teachingtimes.com/bookshop/product/emotional-literacy-assessment-and-intervention-11-16/?srsltid=AfmBOoo8w SX1yKpWRGf4Y6ip-iJuArzwH_EYEQri_6R-fndktP8clGEb

Appendix M

SEND Status	PP Indicator	CAT Mean	CAT Quantitative	CAT Spatial	CAT Non-Verbal	CAT Verbal	Reading Y7	Reading Current	Spelling Y7	Working Memory % Processing Difficulties	Emotional Literacy Y7	EL Current	Exam Arrangements	Comments
K, C&L	Y	92	95	88	94	90	8.1	10.11	8.04	13*	80			SpLD: dyslexic/dispraxic characteristics
K, C&L	Y	86	85	81	87	91	7.01	10.07	8.04	9**	78		ET	SLCN/SpLD characteristics
K, SEMH	Y	106	103	102	90	89	15.06	n/a	10.07	79	70		ICT, ET	ADHD (medicated), ASD characteristics
K, C&L, C&L		82	71	89	92	75	6.05	8.06	7.1	45**	73		ICT, ET	ASD diagnosis, SpLD: dyscalculic/dyslexic characteristics
E, PD, SEMH, C&L		81	81	73	77	92	13.09	13.09		39	48**	61*	ICT, ET, Scribe	DCD, Kinship care, CAMHs, Therapy
K, SEMH, C&L	Y	85	71	87	91	89	8.06	10.11	9.08	68*	58**	68	ICT	LAC, SpLD: dyscalculic characteristics, Therapy
K, C&L	Y	97	84	97	109	96	9.03	12.09	9.02	86**	67		ICT	SpLD: dyslexic/dyscalculic characteristics
E, SEMH, C&L	Y	91	93	73	90	106	10.07	14.06	8.09	66**	66*	69	ET	ADHD characteristics, SpLD Visual Memory 2%
K, SEMH		95	91	98	95	94	12.03	13.09	13.01	50	64*	60**	ICT	High anxiety, seat with — or —
K, C&L		81	81	80	74	88	8.06	10.03	9.06	27*	71			MLD characteristics
K, C&L	Y	97	84	97	109	96	9.03	12.09	9.02	86**	67		ICT	SpLD: dyslexic/discalculic characteristics

DATA TRACKER EXTRACT (ANONYMISED)

KEY: E = EHCP; K = SEN Support; C = Concerns-monitor; *Below Average; **Well Below Average.

C&L = Cognition & Learning: Includes Specific Learning Difficulties (SpLD), e.g. Dyslexia, Discalulia, Moderate Learning Difficulties C&I; C&I = Communication & Interaction: Includes Speech & Language (SLCN) and Autism Spectrum (ASD); SEMH = Social, Emotional & Mental Health: Includes Attention Deficit (ADHD), Attachment Disorder (AD), Well Below Average self-esteem, Anxiety; PD = Physical Disabilities: Includes Visual or Hearing impaired, Developmental Coordination disorder (DCD), Medical needs; LAC = Looked After Child; PP = Pupil Premium.

- On *bespoke registers*, teachers need to view only the most recent scores in competencies such as reading comprehension or emotional literacy.
- Re-testing in any category is unnecessary for students with average level scores or who progress to expected levels.
- Working memory and processing scores are unlikely to change although it may be beneficial to re-test students with emotional or mental health difficulties which can impact memory and processing capacity.
- Exam access arrangements indicate the normal method of working for relevant students, useful for teachers to know.

Index